SACRED WISDOM

THE
PRINCIPAL
UPANISHADS

The Essential Philosophical
Foundation of Hinduism

Alan Jacobs

Introduction by David Frawley

WATKINS PUBLISHING
LONDON

This translation of *The Principal Upanishads* is published by
agreement with O Books/John Hunt Publishing Ltd

This edition produced in 2007 for Sacred Wisdom,
an imprint of Watkins Publishing
Sixth Floor, Castle House, 75–76 Wells Street, London W1T 3QH
Distributed in the United States and Canada by
Sterling Publishing Co., Inc.
387 Park Avenue South, New York, NY 10016-8810

1 3 5 7 9 10 8 6 4 2

Designed in Great Britain by Jerry Goldie
Typeset in Great Britain by Dorchester Typesetting Group
Printed and bound in Thailand by Imago

Library of Congress Cataloging-in-Publication data available

ISBN-10: 1-905857-08-X
ISBN-13: 978-1-905857-08-1

www.watkinspublishing.com

For information about custom editions, special sales, premium
and corporate purchases, please contact Sterling Special Sales
Department at 800-805-5489 or specialsales@sterlingpub.com

CONTENTS

INTRODUCTION

The Upanishads are the primary source book of the profound spiritual wisdom of India going back well before the age of the Buddha some 2,500 years ago. They have provided an ongoing stream of inspiration for the great gurus of the region from the ancient to the modern eras. From the teachings of Krishna in the Bhagavad Gita to those of modern masters like Sri Aurobindo and Ramana Maharshi, Upanishadic insights have remained shining brightly, like an inextinguishable fire, at the core of the soul of India.

The Upanishads mediate between the mantric visions of the ancient Vedic seers and the meditative insights of later yogic sages. They show us the mystical side of the Vedic world and its luminous images of the cosmic fire and the cosmic sun as the supreme light of awareness. Yet they also delineate a logical philosophical approach to truth based on a clear articulation of the ideas of God, the Self and the Absolute.

There is little in the spiritual wisdom of India that does not have its counterpart or seed in the Upanishads. For those who want to discover the real spiritual roots of the Yoga tradition, the Upanishads remain crucial as they first clearly explain the practice of yoga in all of its major forms, the harmonization of body, breath and mind for the realization of the inner Spirit or Purusha. Yet we also find in the Upanishads the seeds of the

Buddhists' ideas of the supremacy of the mind and the need for deep introspection. Whether it is the law of karma, the process of rebirth, the different bodies of the soul, the practice of meditation, mantra, pranayama, the idea of dharma or natural law, these can all be found in beautiful Upanishadic verses.

Yet the Upanishads are relevant if not central to world spirituality, not just to students of the traditions of India. Indeed, if one combines the theism and devotion of Western religions with the formless meditation and impersonal views of Eastern religions, one would end up with something similar to the Upanishadic teachings which embrace both theism and monism.

The Upanishads teach monism, that all is God or the Absolute, *Sarvam Khalvidam Brahma*, "Everything is Brahman". But they do not do this in simply an abstract manner. That One Being is present in all of us as our own deeper and immortal soul and Self, the Atman, *Aham Brahmasmi*, "I am Brahman" or the Absolute. In this regard, the Upanishads probably first clearly set forth in human history a way of Self-Knowledge taking us to the Absolute. Yet theism is also present in many places in the Upanishads, a recognition of One God or Isvara as the creator, preserver and destroyer of the universe and the ability to unite with Him (or Her) through meditation. The Upanishads also say *Ishavasyam Idam Sarvam*, "All this universe is pervaded by the Lord".

The Upanishads present a marvellous ontology of Being as the foundation, background and goal of all life. The Upanishads also probably first clearly explicate the law of karma and the process of rebirth in rational terms.

The questions raised by the Upanishadic sages remain relevant to all serious thinkers of ultimate truth. They include such deep queries as: "Through knowing what one thing can everything be known?" "By what can the knower be known?" And the deepest of all questions: "Who am I?"

However, the Upanishadic approach is not merely conceptual. It is part of a tradition of *sadhana* or spiritual practice. Upanishadic enquiries into reality proceed through mantra and meditation, not just through logic and sensory perception. Besides its philosophy, the Upanishads outline important spiritual practices. These include the method of Self-Enquiry, meditation (both with form and without form), the chanting of mantras like OM, devotional worship of the divine, and yogic practices like working with the breath.

Alan Jacobs is himself a meditator and a mystic poet. He brings his life experience and deep inner sensitivity into his translation, which is but one of his many forays into the spiritual field. Alan represents a new group of thinkers who find a living inspiration in the Upanishads, those who have been to India, studied with its great gurus, and learned the inner teachings in a direct and experiential manner. This makes his translation unique, appealing and alive and worthy of examination even by those who may already have translations of these great texts.

Many other Upanishadic translations fall short because they are done by scholars who lack the spiritual insight to appreciate the many layers of Upanishadic language, thought and analysis. Alan's transcreation – a free verse poetic rendering – of ten of the principal Upanishads offers a new view, which carries the ancient light and inspiration of the Upanishads forward to the modern reader in the West. Contemplating his renditions elevates the mind, heart and soul of the reader.

At this time in world history, an examination of Upanishadic thought is important. It will help connect us to the deeper roots of unitary thought and awareness at the heart of our greater world spirituality, the heritage of the ancient seers and sages whose guidance we need today more so than ever.

David Frawley
Author *Yoga and the Sacred Fire, Vedantic Meditation*

THE ISA UPANISHAD

Introduction

This Upanishad is traditionally placed first in the edition of the twelve Upanishads[1] chosen by the great Shankaracharya for his commentaries. Juan Mascaro,[2] the Spanish poet, in his fine translation says that it is an ancient tradition to place this Upanishad first. It comes from the Yajur Veda. William Butler Yeats, the important Anglo-Irish poet, also places it first in his translation.[3]

1.   All is perfect, so perfectly perfect!
     Whatever being lives, moves
     And breathes on Earth
     At every level from atom
     To galaxy is absolutely perfect in its place
     Precise and choreographed,
     Because "That" flows from the Glory of God,
     The Lord,
     The Self,
     Consciousness,
     The Source,
     Awareness, Peace, and Love,
     And is therefore perfect.
     When you have surrendered your ego

To "That"
You will find true happiness.
Never ever envy the place of
Any other man or woman.

Mahatma Gandhi regarded this verse as one of the most important in Indian scripture.

Many people shy at the concept of "everything is perfect". This is stated from a cosmic standpoint where in a holistic universe every thing has its place to maintain balance and harmony of the whole. It is not an anthropomorphic humanistic view of what happens on earth by itself. To the man or woman totally surrendered to God everything which happens must be accepted as perfect even if it is not understood or approved of from the egotistic individual's standpoint.

2. Although a man or woman may desire
To live for a hundred years
Performing good deeds,
No other way than this total surrender,
Acceptance of "what is"
Shall stop these deeds
From binding him or her.

3. There are the worlds of the ignorant
And the wicked,

Hypnotized in blind darkness.
Those who have lost hold
Of Knowledge of their True Self,
Of Consciousness, Reality, Love,
They return after death
To various levels of existence,
In the vast universe
As Consciousness ordains.

4. That One, the True Self
Of Consciousness, Reality, Love,
Although still,
Is swifter than thought,
As a greyhound is to a tortoise.
The senses never know "That".
Consciousness runs and overtakes them.
Without "That Self" there is no
Real Life, I assure you.

5. Consciousness
Moves and does not move,
It appears to be distant
Yet is near,
It animates all
And envelopes all,
Eternally.

6. Who sees "all being"
   In his or her own Self
   As Consciousness, Awareness,
   Like his own Self,
   Never suffers from fear.

7. When a man or woman
   Understands and knows
   That the Self of Consciousness
   Reality, Love,
   Has become all that exists,
   What possible trouble or sorrow
   Can affect
   He or she who has seen
   That seamless Unity?

8. This Self of Consciousness
   Encircles all,
   Bright,
   Luminous,
   Formless,
   Transparent,
   Pure,
   Unembellished.
   Like the sage,
   Wise, Self-Existent,
   All knowing.

"That" establishes perfect order
Righteously for all time.

This echoes Krishna's promise in the Gita to restore the dharma whenever the world falls below a certain level of balanced harmony, as at present. The advents of Ramana Maharshi and Ramakrishna in the 20th century are therefore highly significant in this respect.

9. Any man or woman
    Who worships
    What is not True, Good,
    From the Self alone,
    But follows blind action
    Without Knowledge,
    Drops into the pit of darkness,
    As do those who only follow Knowledge
    Without wise action.

Paradoxically even wise knowledge fails without wise action, the karma yoga of surrender and renunciation, the acceptance of "what is".

10. Knowledge alone has
     A disastrous outcome,
     As does action alone,
     So we have learned from

The inspired Sage Wisdom
Of the Ancient Rishis.

11. But he who understands
The wisdom of Self-Knowledge,
Jnana Yoga
And the wisdom of Action,
Karma Yoga
And the wisdom of Surrender,
Bhakti Yoga
Overcomes even death
And with this understanding
Reaches the level beyond time into Immortality.

Time is a lower level of existence, a consequence of maya. As Kant and Schopenhauer pointed out, it is an "a priori concept" in the brain or organ of cognition and has no substantial reality; it creates maya. The man who combines the wisdom of jnana, karma and bhakti yoga, transcends the time sequence in this life and after. He lives in the power of the eternal now.

12. Into deep darkness fall
Those who worship only
The Immanent in the body,
And to greater darkness

Fall those who worship
Only the Transcendent Spirit.

This is another paradoxical warning against half-baked understanding. True worship must be paid to the divine Immanence in the microcosmic Self as well as the divine transcendent Spirit in the macrocosmic universe. Unless the two are understood as One, not two, disaster falls as with most dualistic comprehension which is very limited and only a stepping stone to non-duality (Advaita).

13. So worship of the
   Immanent without the
   Worship of the Transcendent
   Leads to different consequences.
   This we have learned from
   The Ancient Rishis
   And the primeval sage
   Dakshinamurti
   Who taught by silence.

14. Men and women who
   Truly worship the God in their own Selves
   And the God of the Whole Universe,
   Reach the level of Immortality
   Beyond Time.

15. The Face of Truth,
    Of the Inner Self,
    The Divine Inner Eye,
    The Sat-Guru within,
    Is veiled by a Golden Light.
    We pray that the
    Supreme Spirit
    May reveal the whole Truth to us,
    Unveiled, in its full glory,
    Before we die.

16. Oh Supreme Spirit –
    Nourisher,
    Controller of all,
    Illuminating Light,
    Fountain of Life
    For all beings –
    Withhold thy blinding light,
    Gather in thy rays,
    So we may see,
    Through thy Grace
    The blessed formulation,
    The Divine,
    That which dwells within us,
    Is "That Being"
    "That" am I.

17. Allow my life
    Through thy Grace
    To merge as One
    In thy All Pervading Life.
    Ashes are to be the end
    Of my body. AUM!
    Oh mind at the point of death
    Remain fixed on Brahman,
    Remember, remember, this,
    Please, I beg you.

This injunction is echoed in the Gita as advice at the point of death. Brahman is the formless highest conception of God, Self, Consciousness, Spirit, Awareness, Peace and Love. It would be an error to drug an advanced soul with anesthetics at the point of death. He should remain fully conscious to move on in his adventure in Consciousness.

18. Oh Divine Agni
    Lead us to peace
    And happiness.
    You know us completely
    In thought and deed.
    Preserve us from the sham
    Deceitful allure of Maya,
    World illusion.

> To you we offer obeisance
> Again and again and again.

These last two verses are often said as prayers before death. Agni is the sacred fire of God which is an intermediary between Brahman (Supreme Spirit) and mankind.

This Upanishad is capable of great mystical interpretation. One may read the inspired commentaries of Sri Aurobindo or Ganapati Muni for such yogic insights on this Upanishad.

THE KENA UPANISHAD

Introduction

The first word of this Upanishad is Kena (By Whom?) and comes from the Sama Veda. It describes the Supreme as Absolute Brahman, and then subsequently the Supreme as God or Isvara. It stresses that the highest teaching (the *para vidya*) leading to Self-Realization is possibly only for those who can control their minds to some extent and have powers of inward concentration. The lower teaching (*apara vidya*) of Isvara sets one on the way leading eventually to the *para vidya*. "By Whom?" presages the vital Self-Enquiry of Ramana Maharshi. Shankara made the distinction between the two *vidyas* in his *Commentary on the Bhagavad Gita* and elsewhere.

Part 1

1. The Seeker enquires:
   At whose wish does the mind
   Wander so far?
   At whose wish does the body exist?
   At whose wish does the tongue speak,
   What God commands
   The eye with its gift of colour
   Or the ear with its gift of sound?

2. The Teacher answers:
   It is the Self, Brahman,
   As Consciousness, Reality, Love,
   Which is the ear of the ear,
   Mind of the mind,
   Speech of the speech,
   Breath of the breath
   And eye of the eye.
   Once one surrenders false
   Identification of the Self with body-mind
   But sees the Self as Consciousness,
   Awareness, with the senses
   And the brain as servants,
   Then freed from the senses and brain,
   The wise know the Self as Consciousness
   To be none other than the formless
   Unqualified Absolute Brahman;
   At death the wise ones transcend
   This world of relative time
   And enjoy Eternity.

3. On this plane the eye does not see,
   The tongue does not wag idly,
   Nor the mind grasp mindlessly,
   The whole nature of Brahman
   We neither understand
   Nor are able to teach, alas.

4. Different is Brahman from the known,
   Different too from the unknown,
   So the Ancient Rishis tell us.

5. That which cannot be
   Expressed in words
   But by which the tongue speaks
   "That" is Brahman,
   Not the God the people
   Worship in ignorance.[4]

6. "That" which does not
   Think by the brain
   But by which the brain thinks,
   "That" is Brahman.
   Brahman is not the God
   Worshipped by men and women,
   I assure you.

7. That which does not see by the eye
   But the power by which the eye sees,
   "That" is Brahman,
   Not the God worshipped by the people,
   I assure you.

8. "That" which does not
   Hear by the ear
   But the power by which
   The ear hears,
   "That" alone is Brahman,
   Not the God that men
   And women adore,
   I assure you.

9. "That" which does not
   Breathe by the breath,
   But the power by which
   The breath is drawn,
   "That" alone is Brahman,
   Not the God that people praise,
   I assure you.

Part 2

1. The Teacher says:
   If you think you know this well
   Then you know very little.
   What is known by you
   Is only the appearance of Brahman
   That strikes the senses.
   So continue with your studies,
   My dear sons and daughters.

2. The Seeker answers:
   I do not think I understand it well,
   Nor do I understand that
   I do not understand it either.

The paradoxical use of the double negative is a device
frequently employed in Advaitic texts. Here it is emphasized,
with humour. Zen Buddhists also enjoy the use of paradoxical
teaching where the metaphysical clashes with the empirical.
But all is One – samsara is nirvana. The world is an appearance
in Brahman, of which Brahman is the substratum.

3. To he or she
   It is not understood,
   To he or she it is
   Understood,
   To whom it is
   Understood
   He does not understand.
   It is not understood
   By those who
   Understand it.
   It is understood
   By those who do
   Not understand it.
   He or she who truly understands
   Brahman knows that

"That" is beyond knowledge.
He or she who thinks he or she knows
Does not know.
The ignorant believe that
Brahman can be known.
The Rishis know that
"That" is beyond knowledge.

The paradox is re-emphasized. We are in the realm of the Buddhist "koan".

4. "That" is known by
    The awakening of Enlightenment
    Or Self-Realization.
    Then we surmount
    Worldly time as on a mountain peak
    And live in the Eternal Now.

5. By Self-Realization we
    Gain strength, knowledge
    And Immortality.
    If a man or woman
    Understands this fully
    "That" is the supreme goal of life.
    If he does not know "That"
    Then there is transmigration
    Into other births.

The Rishis who have earnestly
Meditated on the nature of "That"
And seen the Self as
Consciousness, Reality, Love,
In all and everything,
Become deathless
When they leave the body.

Part 3

1. Brahman won the war between
    The Good Gods and Wicked Demons.
    The Gods were elated by their triumph,
    But foolishly claimed this victory for themselves.

We now move to a literary mythological diversion, a story that contains concealed metaphysical truth. There is struggle between egotism and altruism at every level of the universe. Brahman is all powerful and inscrutable, and always victorious.

2. Brahman apperceived this
    And appeared to them,
    But they failed to recognize
    "That"
    And communed with this
    And asked what it was?

3. So the Gods consulted
    Agni, God of Sacred Fire,
    And asked him to find out
    What this Spirit was.
    Agni agreed to co-operate,
    Not reluctantly.

4. He ran towards the Spirit.
    Brahman asked him who
    He was.
    He replied:
    "I am Agni, God of Sacred Fire."

5. Brahman enquired:
    "What power is in you?"
    Agni said he could
    Burn everything there was
    On Earth, entirely
    With one flash.[5]

6. Brahman put a single
    Straw before him,
    And asked him to burn it.
    Agni strained with all
    His entire might but failed
    To set it alight.
    He returned to the Gods downcast.

7. Then they asked Vayu,
   God of the Air,
   "Oh Vayu – find out what this Spirit is."
   Vayu agreed, not with reluctance.

8. He ran towards it
   And Brahman asked:
   "Who are you?"
   He answered,
   "I am Pneumatic Vayu, God of Air
   And Winds."

9. Brahman asked:
   "What Power have you?"
   Vayu answered:
   "I could sweep all things
   That exist on Earth
   Away with one puff."

10. Brahman put the same
    Straw before him.
    "Now lift it up," he said.
    Vayu advanced with all his might,
    Blowing, huffing, puffing furiously
    But it refused to shift.
    So he returned to the Gods, crestfallen,

Saying, "I could not find
Out what kind of Spirit this is, alas."

11.   Then they said to
Indra, Mighty King of all the Gods,
"Please find out what
Spirit this is."
He went towards it but
It vanished before his eyes.

12.   Then in that same space
Indra came towards
A very beautiful woman,
Highly bejewelled,
And smelling sweetly
Of perfumed fragrance.
It was Uma, wife of
Lord Shiva,
Daughter of Himarat,
Once known as Parvati.
Indra asked "Who is
This Spirit?"
"I shall enquire."

Part 4

1. The fair Uma answered:
    "Surely you realize 'That' is
    Brahman.
    It is only through his victory
    That you have all become magnificent."
    Then Indra too recognized
    "That" Consciousness was Brahman, indeed.

2. So Agni, God of Fire, Vayu,
    God of Air, and Indra, King of the Gods
    Excelled the lesser Gods
    Because now they too recognized
    The Supreme Absolute Brahman,
    As "That" Consciousness, Self, Awareness,
    Love, Peace.

3. Indra was now truly King,
    Above all the other Gods, for he
    Was the first to know Brahman!

4. This is the mythological
    Teaching of Brahman with
    Regards to the other Gods.
    It is that recognition which flashes
    Forth in forked lightning

From a dark cloud
And then disappears,
Like a thunderbolt.

5. And this is Brahman's
Teaching in relation
To men and women: he is found
In the motion of the mind,
That power which moves
The mind in Brahman, Consciousness.
On this revelation men and women should
Earnestly
Meditate day and night.

6. Brahman, Consciousness, Self, Peace, Love,
Is the adorable power in all beings,
He who meditates upon him as such
Is honoured by all beings for ever.

7. The Devotee asked
To be told more about Brahman.
The Teacher replied: "You have
Been told the Secret Knowledge,[6]
The nature of Brahman, as
Consciousness, Reality, Self, Love,
In this Upanishad.

8. The feet on which this
    Upanishad stands
    Are austerity, mind control
    And acceptance of 'what is'.
    The Sacred Vedas are its limbs,
    Truth is its happy home,
    Garlanded by the Gods.

9. He who sees
    The meaning of this Upanishad
    And has cast off all wickedness
    Stands in the Infinite,
    Supreme plane of heaven.
    Yes in the plane of heaven.
    AUM, peace, peace, peace,
    For ever and ever."

THE KATHA UPANISHAD

Introduction

The Katha Upanishad belongs to the Yajur Veda. It starts with a popular story well known in ancient Sanskrit literature, that of the boy hero, Naciketas. Naciketas asks the Lord of Death to be told about the mystery of enlightenment. There are echoes of this popular Upanishad in the Bhagavad Gita. Sir Edwin Arnold, the celebrated Victorian poet who versified the Gita and the *Life of the Buddha (The Light of Asia)*, also versified this Upanishad under the title *The Secret of Death*.

BOOK I

Part 1

1. Vagasravasa,
   Father of Naciketas
   Yearned for heavenly rewards
   So he sacrificially surrendered everything
   He owned.

2. When the promised gifts
   Were handed to the Brahmins
   Faith entered the heart of
   His young son Naciketas;
   He pondered:

3. "Worthless must be worlds
   To which a man thinks he goes,
   Just for presenting gifts of barren cows."

4. Then realizing that his father
   Was giving up all he had to the Brahmins
   He asked him what he proposed
   To give to him, his son.
   Receiving no reply he asked twice more.
   Vagasravasa roared angrily,
   "If you don't keep quiet
   I shall hand you over to Yama,
   God of Death!
   That will be your reward!"

5. Naciketas mildly replied, "As you wish, Father,
   I shall go as the first,
   Leading many who are all
   Sooner or later destined to die.
   Many are dying at this moment, as we speak.
   What shall be the deeds of Yama,

> Ruler of the Kingdom of Death,
> What can he do to me – today?

6. I reflect on how it was with those
   Who came to Death before,
   How it will be with those
   Who come hereafter.

Meditation on death is one of the most powerful means of awakening. Ramana Maharshi, who was Self-Realized at the age of sixteen, meditated on death after he lost his father and became enlightened. George Gurdjieff stressed the need for men and women to contemplate their own death to wake up from "sleep". J. Krishnamurti was profoundly affected by the death of his brother at a young age and it led to an awakening. Gerald Manley Hopkins wrote an eloquent prose meditation on death for his fellow Jesuits. These are only a few examples of very many in the spiritual life:

> A mortal slowly ripens
> Like golden corn in a brown field.
> He or she then withers,
> But springs up again.

Naciketas entered into the Kingdom of Yama but Yama was not there to welcome him. Then one of his servants apologetically said to the boy:

7. "Fire sweeps the house
   When a man of Brahman
   Comes as a guest,
   And is not welcomed.
   Fire can only then be quenched
   By a peace offering of water.

8. A man of Brahman
   Who lives in the house of a fool
   Without being offered food
   Will destroy his hopes and wishes,
   His goods, his goodness,
   His sense of sacredness,
   Worthy deeds,
   And all his sons and cattle!"
   So Lord Yama eventually
   Returned after three nights away,
   During which time Naciketas
   Had received no hospitality.

9. Lord Yama spoke:
   "Oh boy of Brahman
   You are a worthy guest,
   You have stayed in my house
   For three whole nights
   Without any food
   So you may choose three boons.
   Victory to thee and eternal well-being to you."

10. Naciketas pondered
    And replied:
    "Oh Lord Yama
    Of the three boons
    You have graciously granted.
    I firstly choose that my dear father
    Vagasravasa be pacified
    And is freed from anger
    Towards me,
    And that he may know me
    And greet me
    When you send me back."

11. Yama replied:
    "Through my Grace
    Your father
    Will know you,
    Be freed from wrath.
    He will sleep well,
    Especially when I free you
    From my yawning mouth.
    Ah!"

12. Naciketas replied:
    "In heaven there is no fear
    Because there is no death,
    No old age,

No hunger and thirst,
No sorrow,
All rejoice there.

13.   You know, Lord Yama,
      The Vedic Fire Sacrifice
      Leads us heavenward.
      Teach me, I am full of faults.
      Those who live in heaven are Immortal,
      This is the second boon
      I wish to receive."

14.   Lord Yama answered:
      "I will tell it to you
      And when you understand
      The significance of the Fire Sacrifice,
      Which leads to heaven,
      Know it is the attainment
      Of infinite worlds
      And their firm support
      Veiled in darkness."

15.   Yama then taught him
      The ways and meanings
      Of the Fire Sacrifice,
      The beginnings of all worlds,
      The bricks required for the altar,

Their number,
Their placing.
Naciketas repeated it precisely,
Then Yama being pleased said:

16. "I am satisfied with you, my boy,
So I grant thee another boon,
The Fire Sacrifice shall be renamed
The Naciketas Sacrifice.
Take this necklace of jewels.[7]

17. He who performs this
Rite three times
And has been reunited with
His father, mother, and teacher,
And has performed (the three duties:
Study,
Austerity,
Giving to charity,)
Overcomes both birth and death.
When he has learned
And understood the truth of this fire
Which knows
And makes us know
All that is born from Brahman,
Consciousness,

Ancient and Divine,
He reaches Eternal Peace.

18. He who knows the three Naciketas Fires
    And keeps up the sacrifice,
    Having cast off all
    The iron fetters of death,
    Rejoices in heaven
    Beyond grief and sorrow.

19. This then Naciketas
    Is the fire that ceases to leave,
    Which you have chosen
    As your second boon,
    That fire all men will acclaim.
    What is your third boon?"

20. Naciketas said:
    "There is some doubt
    When a man dies,
    Some claiming he is conscious
    Some claiming he is no longer conscious.
    Please teach me the Truth about death.
    This my third wish for a boon."

21. Lord Yama answered:
    "On this point even the Gods
    Have doubts.
    It is hard to understand
    And very, very subtle.
    Choose another boon
    Do not press me
    Let me off this barbed hook."

22. "Ah!" said Naciketas,
    "On this point even Gods have doubts.
    And you have said
    It is hard to understand.
    There is no other teacher like you.
    So no other boon will
    Grant me satisfaction."

23. Lord Yama pleaded:
    "Please choose sons and
    Grandsons who will live for
    A hundred years,
    Great herds of cattle,
    Wives,
    Elephants,
    Gold,
    Horses,
    Anything you crave for on Earth

And live for as many harvests
As you wish.

24. Choose wealth
And a long life, Naciketas.
Be King over the whole Earth.
I will make you happy,
Enjoyer of all possible desires.

25. Whatever desires
Difficult to attain by mortals,
Ask for them as you wish.
Beautiful young virgins
Riding in their own golden chariots,
Playing sitars and veenas,
Be waited upon by them,
Consoled by them.
But please do not ask
Me about the mystery of death
I implore you!"

26. "Oh Yama
These trifling baubles
Only last an hour,
They wear out man's strength
And aggravate the senses.
Life is too short!

Keep horses, dancing virgins,
And songs for your own pleasure,
Not for mine.

27.   No man has ever been
Made happy by riches
And sensual pleasures alone.
Who wants to be wealthy?
Only fools.
When I see you
Who can live as long
As you rule?
Only that boon
I have chosen
Will satisfy my desire for Truth.

28.   What greater knowledge
For a mortal
Slowly perishing here below,
Knowing after talking with thee
The freedom from decay
Enjoyed by Immortals;
Nothing else could delight me
After I have weighed up
The noxious vanity
Which arises from physical beauty,
And carnal passion?

29.   No, no, no,
      What is that on which hangs the
      Great Doubt,
      Oh Lord of Death?
      Tell me what there is
      In the great Hereafter?
      This boon
      I have chosen
      Will satisfy my desire
      For Truth,
      Nothing else.
      I will not choose
      Any other boon
      But that which penetrates
      Into the Veiled, Hidden
      World existing beyond
      My brain and senses."

Part 2

1.   Yama started to teach Naciketas.
     "The Good is one thing,
     Pleasure is another.
     These two have different aims,
     They bind a man or woman
     In cords of attachment.
     It goes well with him or her

Who clings to the Good,
But he who chooses Pleasure
Is like an arrow which
Misses the mark.[8]

2. The Good and Pleasurable
   Both woo men and women, continuously.
   The wise circumnavigate
   Them and distinguish one from
   The other very clearly.
   The wise prefer the Good
   To the Pleasurable, the fool
   Chooses what is Pleasurable,
   Driven by greed, lust and indulgence.

3. You, my boy, Naciketas,
   After pondering on all pleasures
   That either are or appear to be delightful
   Have wisely dismissed them all.
   You have not wandered on
   To the rotten potholed road that leads
   To wealth on which so many
   Men stumble and are then run over.

4. Leagues apart,
   Leading to different ends
   Are these two,
   One I call ignorance,
   The second I call Wisdom.
   I can see that you are one
   Who seeks Knowledge,
   For even the temptation
   Of great pleasures
   Did not pull you away.[9]

5. Fools dwelling in darkness,
   Wise, only in their own arrogance,
   Puffed up with false pride and beliefs,
   Go round and round in circles
   Staggering like the blind
   Led by the blind, into ditches,
   Or chasing their own tails like bitches,
   Seduced by power and lust for riches.

6. Knowledge of the Hereafter never arises
   Before the eyes of a careless fool
   Deluded by the delusion of riches.
   'This is the only world,' he thinks,
   'There is no other.'
   So he falls again and again
   Under my sway.

7. 'That', the Self of Consciousness,
   Of whom many are not even aware,
   And when they are told
   Fail to understand.
   Wonderful is a Sage when found
   Who is capable of bringing
   Him or her to Self-Knowledge.
   Wonderful too is he or she
   Who realizes the Self of Consciousness
   When taught by an able Master.

8. That same Self when
   Taught by an inferior
   So-called 'Guru'
   Is hard to comprehend
   Even when thought about often.
   Unless it be taught by a Sage
   There is no way to understanding,
   For it is subtler than the subtle.

9. This teaching will not
   Be understood
   Through argument,
   But when declared by
   One who knows.
   Then, dear boy, it is easy
   To understand.

You have now seen 'That',[10]
You are truly a boy of resolution.
May all seekers be like you!"

10.   Naciketas replied:
      "I know what men and women
      Call treasure is the transient,
      Like a soap bubble in the wind,
      The Eternal cannot be won
      By that which is not Eternal.
      Hence the sacred Vedic Fire of Sacrifice
      Has been laid by me first.
      Thus by means of the transient
      I have comprehended 'what is'
      Existence,
      Not transient phenomena.
      'That' is
      The Teaching of Yama."

Advaita (non-duality) teaches that there is no incompatibility
between the empirical and the transempirical or metaphysical;
because Brahman, which is transempirical or metaphysical, is
the ground or substratum of the empirical, there cannot be
any contradiction or incompatibility between the ground and
the grounded. S. Radhakrishnan says this verse reminds him
of William Blake: "To see a world in a grain of sand, and a
heaven in a wild flower; hold infinity in the palm of your

hand, and eternity in an hour." We have to use the empirical world of the senses to attain to the realm of the metaphysical. Samsara and nirvana are One, as the Buddha stated – a remark often quoted by the Mumbai sage Ramesh Balsekar.

11. Yama spoke:
     "Although you have seen the
     Fulfilment of all desires,
     The Source of the world,
     The endless rewards for good deeds,
     The other shore where fear does not exist.
     All that is glorified by worship,
     The wide heavens,
     The resting place in the Source;
     Yet being wise
     You have thrown away such conceptual
     Knowledge.

12. The Wise who continually cognize their
     Self as Consciousness, Reality, Love,
     Sat, Chit, Ananada,
     Recognize 'That' as the Source,
     Hard to be perceived
     Yet transparently obvious,
     Hidden in the darkness of the body,
     Dwelling in the cave of the Heart,
     Living on the edge of an abyss,

Realizing 'That' as God, the Source,
He leaves the dual opposites, joy and sorrow,
Far behind.

13. An earnest, receptive man or woman
    Who has heard this and seen it
    Has separated his or her Consciousness or Self
    From the mind-body organism
    And has reached the subtlety
    Of his or her own Being.
    He or she rejoices
    Because he or she has reached
    The cause of all rejoicing.
    The doorway of the House of Brahman
    Now lies open before you, my dear Naciketas."

14. Naciketas asked Yama:
    "That which you see as
    Neither this nor that,
    As neither cause nor effect,
    As neither past nor future,
    What does that mean?"

15. Yama replied:
    "That word to which all Vedas point,
    To which all austerities lead,
    Which all men and women desire

Who thirst after righteousness,
Which they try to live
As spiritual seekers,
That word is AUM.

The Mandukya Upanishad, which is the foundation of the
Advaita system established in Gaudapada's *Karika*
(commentary), enlarges on the meaning of AUM. Shankara
was his pupil and has commented both on the *Karika* and the
Upanishad.

16. That eternal sacred syllable
     Signifies the Absolute
     Supreme Brahman,
     He who comprehends
     The sound and meaning of
     AUM
     Truly understands Self-Realization.

17. AUM is the best support,
     AUM is the highest support,
     He who chants this support
     Is magnified.

18. The knowing Self
    As Consciousness-Awareness
    Is not born,
    It never dies,
    It sprang from No Thing
    No Thing sprang from 'That'.
    This Ancient, Primordial Consciousness
    Inherent in every being is Eternal
    It is not slain even when the body dies.

This is echoed in the Bhagavad Gita, II: 19–20.

19. If the killer believes he or she kills,
    If the killed believes that he or she
    Has been killed,
    They fail to understand,
    For no individual actually kills
    Nor is any individual ever killed.

This cryptic verse points to the understanding that the Self is deathless and the slayer of the body preordained by destiny. This is discussed by Lord Krishna in Chapter II of the Gita with Arjuna.[11]

20. The Self,
     Smaller than the smallest,
     Greater than the greatest,
     Is hidden in the Heart of every Being.
     A man or woman free
     From desires and suffering
     Knows the majesty of the Self
     As Consciousness, Reality, Love,
     Through Divine Grace.

The Self is beyond measure – Consciousness is infinite and everywhere. Ramana Maharshi pointed out that the Self is the true heart of all beings and is recognized through grace.

21. Though sitting still
    He travels far,
    Though lying down
    He goes everywhere,
    Who save my Self
    As Consciousness
    Knows 'That' Consciousness,
    Who rejoices,
    And rejoices not?

This verse delights in paradox. The Self is not an object but the ultimate subject of pure Consciousness, Awareness, I-am-ness. Western philosophy reached the same point several thousands of years later with Berkeley, Kant and Schopenhauer. Terence Gray (Wei Wu Wei) and Ramesh Balsekar stress this vital pointer in their books, using similar Kantian language.

22. The Wise who know the Self
    As Consciousness,
    Formless,
    Within the forms,
    Unchanging
    Amongst the changing,
    Omnipresent,
    Never ever suffer.

Yama's teaching on the nature of the Self is clear, unequivocal and uncompromising.

23. That Self
    As Pure Consciousness,
    Awareness,
    Source of Being,
    Cannot be gained
    By merely reading the Vedas
    Nor by pontifical, pedagogical
    Pompous punditry.
    He whom the Self chooses,
    By him or her the Self

> Can be realized.
> The Self chooses their body
> As his own.

The recognition experimentally that the Self is Consciousness comes through grace. The penny drops when the intellect stops trying to get its head around it and the search is called off. Douglas E. Harding's "experiments" are designed to point this out very forcibly, for example, living without a head, etc.

24. But he or she who has not stopped
     Hurting others,
     Who is not serene and quiet,
     Whose mind is still restless,
     Cannot cognize the Self
     As Consciousness
     Even when told.

25. Who then truly knows
     Where he or she is?
     He or she to whom
     The Priests and Warriors
     Are merely impressions
     To be digested as substance for food,
     And death as a spicy seasoning?"

Part 3

1. There are two,
    The Supreme Absolute Brahman,
    And "That's" shadow,
    Enjoying the spectacle
    Of their own works,
    Entering into the Heart Cave,
    Dwelling on the highest peak,
    The Heart's Ether.
    Those who know Brahman
    See the light and its shadow,
    Just as do those householders
    Who dutifully perform
    The Naciketas Fire Sacrifice.

This Upanishad, which is highly literary, now moves into poetical mysticism. The light and shadow anticipate the shadow side in Jungian psychology. The heart centre is central to Ramana Maharshi's teaching. See the *Ramana Gita*, the chapter entitled "Science of the Heart".

2. May we be able to master
    The Naciketas Fire Sacrifice,[12]
    Which is a bridge to the Supreme
    And to the Highest Eternal,
    Absolute Brahman,

For those who wish to cross
Over to the fearless shore.

3. Know the Self
    As your own Consciousness, Awareness,
    Vital Spiritual Life Energy,
    Source of your own Being.
    God in your Heart,
    As if to be sitting as a passenger
    In a golden chariot.
    Your body, an object in Consciousness-Awareness,
    Is the chariot,
    Your subtle intellect
    Is the charioteer,
    And the reasoning power
    Inherent in the brain is the reins.

4. The five wild rampant horses are the senses,
    The objects they perceive
    Are the roads down which they rush headlong.
    When the chariot and charioteer
    Are in Union, that is Yoga
    Of the body,
    The senses,
    The mind.
    Wise people call the Self
    The Enjoyer.

Ramesh Balsekar expands the analogy to cinematography first used by Ramana Maharshi. The silver screen is the organ of cognition illumined by the light of Consciousness (the lamp) on which the film (destiny) appears; the mind-body systems are the destined actors. Consciousness produces, directs, acts all the parts and enjoys the shadow play.

Consciousness produces the movie: there are sixteen frames a second for the sense of time; space for dimension; cause and effect for action. Then colour, sound, smell, touch, and the mental sensations.

As Kant and Schopenhauer pointed out, time, space, and causality are a priori functions in the brain, as is the sense of colour, and produce the maya (the screen for the tragicomic melodrama to take place). This is the sense that the Self is the enjoyer of the action on the screen of Consciousness.

5.　He or she who has no understanding
　　Where reins are not firmly held[13]
　　By the charioteer,
　　Cannot control the wild horses
　　Which become vicious.

6.　But he or she who has
　　Understanding,
　　Whose mind is always firmly held,
　　Has the senses controlled
　　Like the good horses of
　　A noble charioteer.

7.   He who has no understanding,
     Who is unmindful and impure,
     Enters into the cycle
     Of transmigratory births.

8.   He who has understanding,
     Who is mindful, pure,
     Reaches the plane of Eternity.

9.   He who understands,
     His charioteer,
     Holding the reins of the mind,
     Completes his journey, safely.

10. Beyond the senses
     There are the objects,
     Beyond the objects
     The mind,
     Beyond the mind
     Is the intellect.
     The Self
     As Consciousness
     Is beyond the intellect.

For a commentary on the theory of transmigration see my *Transcreation of the Bhagavad Gita* (O Books, John Hunt Publishing, 2003).

11.   Beyond the personal Self
       Is the Potential Energy of Creation,
       Beyond the Potential Energy of Creation
       Is the Source,
       Beyond the Source
       There is No Thing.

This transcreation is influenced by the teaching of Ramana Maharshi and Ramesh S. Balsekar. For an introduction to Ramesh Balsekar's teaching see my *Wisdom of Ramesh Balsekar* (Watkins Publishing, 2003).

12.   The Self, Consciousness,
       In all beings,
       Does not shine,
       But its vacant transparency
       Is seen by subtle seers
       Through their sharp
       Intellect.

The workshops of Douglas E. Harding point to this recognition of the obvious, that Consciousness is subtly separate from the objects perceived. See his masterly book, *Living Without a Head*.

13. A wise man or woman
    Restrains speech
    And the wandering restless
    Monkey mind.
    He should hold them
    In the awareness of
    Consciousness,
    Self-Knowledge,
    And keep quiet.

"Just be quiet" was the advice of H. W. L. Poonjaji (Papaji), sage of Lucknow, disciple of Ramana Maharshi, nephew of Swami Ram Thirta.

14. Arise!
    Awake!
    My boy!
    Having realized your boons
    Let them sink into the depths
    Of your understanding.
    The sharp edge of a razor[14]
    Is more difficult to cross,
    Then the way to a full understanding
    Of Self-Realization,
    Is not easy.

15. He who has seen
    "That",
    Without sound,
    Touch,
    Form,
    Decay,
    Taste,
    Smell,
    Beginning,
    End,
    Beyond All,
    Immutable,
    Eternal,
    Is freed from the yawning jaws
    Of Great Lord Yama, Death.

16. A wise man or woman
    Who has read and
    Studied this ancient tale
    Of Naciketas,
    Told by Lord Yama,
    Is magnified in the realm of
    Brahman.

17. He who repeats this
     Great mystery
     In a Satsang of
     Brahmins,
     Full of devotion,
     Surrendered in Faith,
     Reaches the Infinite.

BOOK II

Part 4

1. Yama spoke to Naciketas:
    "The Source of all Being
    Made the openings
    Of the senses
    So that they turn outward.
    Thus men and women
    Look outward not inward
    Into themselves.
    Some Wise Sage, however, shut his eyes,
    Turned inward,
    And yearning to know the Self,
    Knew the Source of Consciousness
    Deep within his Heart.

2. Children pursue outward pleasures willfully,
    And fall into my spidery web
    Of widespread Death.
    Wise men and women, however, knowing
    The Source of their Immortality,

Stop seeking for stability in a world of instability.

3. 'That' Consciousness,
    Awareness
    Through which we know
    Form,
    Taste,
    Smell,
    Sound,
    Loving touch,
    By 'That' we also can know
    Our own Source of Existence.
    This is the 'That' you have been
    Asked to trace and understand.

4. The Sage
    When he understands
    'That'
    By which he or she sees all
    Forms, both in sleep and waking,
    As the omnipresent
    Self of Consciousness-Awareness
    Suffers no more.

5. He or she who knows
    This living force,
    Which swallows forms
    As the bee sips honey,
    Being Consciousness,

Always near,
Controller of the past and future,
Fears no more.
This is 'That'.

6. 'That', which is the Source
    Manifesting by its own
    Pulsating energy,
    Enters into the Heart,
    Dwells within
    And creates objects from and by the elements.
    This is 'That'.
    He or she who knows
    Aditi,
    That arises with life,
    The essence of the Gods,
    Who, entering the Heart,
    Abides there
    Elemental
    This is 'That'.

Consciousness is the creative impulse to manifest archetypal forms, then elements, which are then rearranged into an infinite variety in multiplicity. This is close to the Platonic Ideas that Schopenhauer utilized in his fusion of mainstream Western philosophy and Upanishadic wisdom, *The World as Will and Idea*.

7. He who understands Aditi,
   The Divine Essence,
   Is One with all Gods
   And arises with the Sacred Prajna,
   All powerful
   Life Breath,
   Who entering into the Heart,
   Lives there
   Elemental,
   This is 'That'.

8. There is Agni,
   Fire,
   All seeing,
   Hidden in the wood
   Before it is rubbed,
   Well guarded
   As a child in the womb
   By its devoted mother.
   Day after day he is to be
   Worshipped
   By men and women when
   They awake and bring offerings.
   This is 'That'.

Agni is close to Prometheus in Western mythology. An intermediary between man and the gods who brings fire to earth and "awakening". Aurobindo's *Hymns of Mystic Fire* extracts the Vedic hymns about Agni in a brilliant translation. They are very powerful devotional aids.

For an understanding of the symbolic meanings of the Vedic gods one should consult the many books of David Frawley, influenced by the Tamil poet-sage-genius, Ganapati Muni. It was the Muni who discovered Ramana Maharshi and then brought him to the notice of the world.

9. And in that Cosmic Dawn
    And Golden Sunset
    All the Gods and Goddesses
    Are contained
    And no one travels beyond,
    This is 'That'.

Here the Upanishad moves from the philosophy of Advaita to the poetic symbolism of the Rig Veda.

10. What is visible in the
     Universe
     Is also invisible in
     Brahman,
     What is there
     Is the same as here.
     He who sees any
     Distinction between Brahman

And the Universe
Transmigrates from death to death.

The microcosm is in the macrocosm, as above so below; these are ancient esoteric ideas. In so far as everything is Consciousness, and Consciousness (Brahman) is all there is, there is no distinction between samsara and nirvana ultimately. The concept of maya is a preliminary pointer to weaken identification with an apparent reality of material forms. Brahman or Consciousness is the substratum of all forms composed of the elements in different juxtapositions.

11. Even by our own mind
     That Brahman as Consciousness
     Can be realized
     Here and now.
     There are no differences,
     Essentially all are One.
     He who thinks there are differences
     Transmigrates from death
     To death in wretched ignorance.

12. The Spirit
     Miniscule, like a thumb,
     Sits in the centre of the body
     As Lord of past and future,
     Knowing all is predetermined

And wholeheartedly accepted as Grace.
Fear ends.

13. That Spirit
Is as a light without smoke,
Lord of the past and future
He is unchanging from day to day.
This is 'That'.

14. As the torrential rains
That fall on a Himalayan mountain slope
Rush down the rocks,
So he or she who perceives
Difference between qualities
And runs after them,
Is like a mad torrent rushing to disaster.

15. As pure crystal water
Poured into pure crystal glass,
The water stays the same.
So the Self is the same
As that of the Seer who has
This understanding."

S. Radhakrishnan in his masterful philosophic commentary on
the Upanishads compares this verse with a saying of St.
Bernard of Clairvaux: "As a drop of water poured into wine

loses itself and takes the colour and savour of wine, so the
saints' human affections dissolve into God's Will."

Part 5

1. "There is a fine city
   With eleven gates
   Of entrance:
   Two eyes,
   Two ears,
   Two nostrils,
   One mouth,
   A navel,
   Two genitalia,
   The Chakra
   At the head's top
   Through which Consciousness rises
   To return to its Source
   After leaving the body.
   This city belongs to
   The Unborn Brahman
   Whose ways are straight.
   He or she who approaches
   The Brahman of Consciousness
   Within the city
   Suffers no more
   And is freed from the bonds of ignorance.
   Such is 'That'.

2. Brahman is the beautiful white swan,[15]
   A Sun shining in the bright heaven,
   He is the air filling the blue sky,
   The red Fire of Sacrifice blazing
   In the hearth,
   He is the guest,
   The divine Soma
   Living in the sacrificial jar.
   He lives in men and women,
   In Gods,
   In sacrifice,
   In heaven.
   He is in water,
   The Earth,
   The mountain.
   He is the True and the
   Magnificent.

3. Brahman exhales
   Sacred breath,
   Who inhales it?
   Continuously creating and
   Dissolving universes
   Over vast eons of time,
   All the Gods praise him,
   The adorable,
   The macrocosm,

The microcosm,
Who dwells in the Heart.

4. When the incarnated
   Brahman
   Lives in the mortal body
   Leaves and is freed
   What remains?
   This is 'That'.

Brahman is the power of Consciousness which leaves the body
on death.

5. No mortal lives
   Simply by exhalation of breath
   Nor inhalation alone.
   We live by 'That'
   Consciousness
   From which both spring
   Effortlessly.

6. I shall now tell you of the mystery
   Of ancient Brahman,
   What happens to the Self of Consciousness after
   Death.

7. Some transmigrate to
   Another womb
   To enjoy form and body,
   Play another part
   In the great drama of Life.
   Others dissolve back into the
   Source,
   Their subtle bodies used
   To form further beings.

8. According to the residual
   Memories of their
   Subtle body experiences
   And their understanding.

9. He is the Sat-Guru
   Who is awake in the Heart
   While we sleep at night
   Forming visions and dramas of delight.
   'That' is indeed the Brahman,
   The bright
   'That' alone is the Immortal Light.
   All universes are contained
   In this great capacity
   No one travels beyond,
   This is 'That'.

10. As the one air,
    Pneumatic,
    After filling space,
    Although One,
    Becomes different
    According to what it enters.
    So is the One Self.
    Consciousness-Awareness
    Within all beings
    Creates differences
    In whatever it enters,
    Within and without.

11. As the magnificent Sun,
    That great golden star
    On the edge of the Milky Way,
    The single eye of the world
    Is unaffected by all
    That takes place,
    Inevitably,
    Under its rays,
    Be it good or bad
    In the eyes of men.
    So the One Self,
    Consciousness,
    In all things
    Is unaffected,

Transcending
World misery,
In the minds of mankind.

12. There is one Ruler,
The Self of Consciousness in all.
The Wise see him within,
To them belong everlasting happiness,
While others, ignorant, needlessly suffer.

13. There is one eternal Doer, thinking,
Yet this thinking,
Is non-doership for him.
He thus fulfils the desires of many.
The Wise who see him
As the Inner Ruler
The Sat-Guru within,
To them belongs everlasting peace,
Not to those who are ignorant."

Naciketas speaks:

14. "They feel highest
Inexpressible bliss
Proclaiming this is 'That',
How can I then understand this mystery?
Is it Self-Effulgent or
Does it reflect light?"

Yama replies:

15. "The Sun does not shine there,
    Nor the silvery Moon of Grace,
    Nor the stars of the myriad galaxies,
    Nor the forked lightning,
    Nor the blazing red fire.
    When Brahman shines
    All shines from him
    By his light – all is 'That'."

Part 6

1. "There is an ancient tree
   The primeval Tree of Life[16]
   Like the Banyan Tree
   With roots shooting up
   And whose branches fall down.
   'That' indeed is the Bright
   The Noble,
   The Brahman,
   The Immortal.
   It has capacity
   For all worlds,
   No one goes beyond her,
   This is 'That'.

2. What ever there is
   In the whole world
   When it emanates from Brahman
   Vibrates in 'That' breath.
   'That' Brahman is a holy terror
   Like a drawn sword.
   Those who know 'That'
   Become Immortal.

3. From fear of Brahman fire rages,
   From terror the Sun burns,
   Even Indra, King of the Gods,
   And Vayu, God of Space,
   And I, Yama, God of Death
   Flee from this awesome power.

4. If a man or woman fails
   To understand Brahman
   Before leaving his or her body,
   Then he or she will transmigrate
   In the worlds of creation,
   According to the form
   That the Will of Brahman decrees.

5. As reflected in a polished mirror,
   So Brahman, the Self,
   The seal of Consciousness,
   May be seen clearly

As transparency
Here within the temple of the body,
Even as if in a dream
In the world of the Ancient Rishis,
As in celestial waters,
In the world of ethereal angels,[17]
As in bright light
And its consequential shadow,
So also in the world of the Creator,
Brahman may be seen.

6. Having seen that the senses
Are distinct from Consciousness
And that waking and sleep
Are part of their existence,
A wise man suffers no more.

7. Behind the senses
Sits the mind-brain,
Beyond that
Is the subtle intellect,
Higher than that is the Self
Of Consciousness, Awareness.
Higher than that the Source
Of all potential energy at rest.

8. Beyond the Source of
   Potential energy at rest
   Is Brahman,
   All pervading, imperceptible.
   All creatures that know 'That'
   Are liberated
   And transcend the time-space illusion,
   And enjoy Eternity.

9. His form is invisible,
   He is visualized
   In the Heart of Wisdom.
   Those who know 'That'
   Transcend the time illusion
   And enjoy Eternity.

10. When the five senses
    Of knowledge
    Stand still
    Along with the mind-brain,
    And when the subtle
    Intellect is unmoving,
    That is the Transcendental State,
    The highest.

11. This reining in of the senses is Yoga.
    The Yogi must be attentive or
    Yoga will come and go.

12. The Self of Consciousness-Awareness
    Cannot be reached by
    Speech,
    By mind-brain
    Or by eye.
    How can it be known
    Except by he or she
    Who realizes
    'That' I am,
    I am 'That'?

13. By the words
    'That' he is
    To be reminded
    And by realizing the reality
    Of both the invisible numinous worlds
    And the visible phenomenal world
    As emanating from Brahman,
    The Source.
    When he apperceives the words
    'I am "That", "That" I am' then 'That',
    Which was there all the time,
    Reveals itself.

These terms phenomenon (the empiric), noumenon (the metaphysical) and apperception (realization) are words derived from Immanuel Kant and Arthur Schopenhauer. They are widely used by Terence Gray (Wei Wu Wei) and the Mumbai sage, Ramesh Balsekar. See my book, *The Wisdom of Ramesh Balsekar* (Watkins Publishing, 2003).

14.　When all desires
　　　Dwelling in the Heart end
　　　Then the mortal becomes Immortal
　　　And understands Brahman.

15.　When all the rope bonds
　　　That knot the Heart are cut,
　　　The mortal becomes Immortal,
　　　Here ends the Highest Teaching.

16.　There are a hundred arteries
　　　Leading from the Heart,
　　　One of them penetrates
　　　The crown of the head.
　　　Moving upwards by this route
　　　A man at death reaches the Eternal.
　　　The other arteries serve
　　　For leaving in other ways.

17.　The Inner Self
　　　Of Consciousness, Awareness,
　　　Is always settled in the Heart.
　　　Let a man or woman draw

Knowledge of that Self
With steady attention
As one draws the pith
From a reed of jungle grass.
Let him realize the Self
As the Bright,
The Immortal,
Yes, as the Bright,
As the Immortal!"

18. Having heard this knowledge
Taught by Lord Yama
And the principles of Yoga,
Naciketas became freed
From his passions and Death,
And realized Brahman
The Self of Consciousness, Awareness.
So it shall be with any other
Who knows "That" which refers to the Self.

19. May Brahman protect us all,
May he enjoy us all,
May we gain strength together,
May our Self-Knowledge brightly shine,
May we cease from disputation,
AUM! Peace! Peace!
Hari Hi, AUM!

THE TAITTIRIYA UPANISHAD

The Taittiriya Upanishad comes from the Yajur Veda. It opens with the science of phonetics and pronunciation. The rishis knew that the precise intonation of each syllable chanted with the whole body had a profound effect on the psyche through listening, sounding and hearing. To this day Upanishads are chanted correctly in some ashrams of India where there are still Vedic schools, such as at Ramanasramam, Tiruvannamalai. Shankara wrote a commentary on this Upanishad. The Upanishad discusses the knowledge of the Supreme Self. Juan Mascaro, Christopher Isherwood and William Butler Yeats only translate extracts, but I prefer to transcreate the entire Upanishad.

BOOK I

Part 1

1. AUM
    May Mitra, God of Prajna, Life Breath, bless us,
    May Varuna, Spirit of the Night,
    Aryaman, Eye of the Sun,
    Indra, Mighty King of the Gods, all bless us.

Brihaspati of Ancient Speech,
And in battle, Vishnu the Great God
Of wide strides bless us.
Hail Brahma, the Creator,
Vayu, Spirit of Air,
All indeed are the visible
Perceptible Brahman!
I shall proclaim righteousness
I shall tell of the True Brahman.
May this prayer protect us
May it protect our Teacher.
AUM!
Peace!
Peace!
Peace!

This verse is from the Rig Veda Samhita. Good health is needed to study the higher wisdom.

The famous yoga teacher B. K. S. Iyengar writes in his treatise, *Light on Yoga*: "The letters AUM depict the three stages of yogic discipline, namely asana, pranayama and *pratyahara*. The entire symbol represents samadhi, the goal for which the three stages are the steps. They represent the triad of Divinity, namely:

Brahma – the Creator
Vishnu – the Maintainer, and
Shiva – the Destroyer of the Universe.

The whole symbol is said to represent Brahman from which the universe emanates, has its growth and fruition and into which it merges in the end. It does not grow or change. Many beings change and pass, but Brahman is the one that always remains unchanged."

The letters AUM also stand for the mantra *Tat Twam Asi*, "That Thou Art", the realization of man's divinity within himself. The entire symbol stands for this realization, which liberates the human spirit from the confines of his body, mind, intellect and ego. The Mandukya Upanishad discusses AUM. Sir Edwin Arnold has versified this Upanishad in his Poem "In an Indian Temple".

Part 2

AUM,
Let us expound Shiksha,
The doctrine of Ancient Vedic
Pronunciation and resonance,
The correct letter,
Accent,
Syllabic quantity,
Effort,
Modulation,
Combination of letters,
This is the lecture.

Part 3

1. May Glory descend to both of us,
   Teacher and Pupil,
   May Vedic light shine upon us!
   Now let us explain the Upanishad,
   The Secret Meaning of the Union
   Under five divisions
   With regard to the worlds,
   The heavenly lights,
   Knowledge,
   Offspring,
   And body derived from Self.
   These are the great Samhitas,
   With regard to the worlds,
   The Earth is the primary element,
   Heaven is the latter element,
   They are united by ether.

This is a mystical cosmology. In the West we have the Kabbalah and Alchemy. They also contain a mystical cosmology and theosophy.

2. That Union also takes place
   Through the expanse of aerial space.

3. With regards to the lights of heaven
   Agni, fire, is the primary element,
   The Sun is secondary,
   Water is their Union.
   The Union occurs through the lightning flash.
   For Knowledge,
   The Teacher is primary,[18]
   The Pupil is secondary,
   Self-Knowledge is their Union,
   It takes place through the
   Correct recitation of the Veda.
   With regard to children,
   The Mother is primary,
   The Father is the latter,
   Offspring are their Union.
   This takes place through
   The planting of the seed in the womb.

4. With regard to
   The body derived from the Self,
   The lower jaw is primary in enunciation,
   The upper jaw is secondary.
   Always relax the jaws.
   Speech is their Union.
   These are the great divisions.
   He who understands
   The significance of these divisions

Becomes blessed
With children, cattle, endless Vedic Light,
Provender and heaven itself.

Part 4

1. May "That"
    The strong bull
    Of the Vedas
    Assuming all forms,
    Who has arisen from the Vedas
    From the Immortal,
    May that Great King of the Gods, Lord Indra,
    Strengthen my Heart with Wisdom.
    May I, Oh Lord, become
    A maintainer of the Immortal.
    May my body prove capable,
    May my tongue be as sweet as acacia honey,
    May I hear all sounds clearly.
    Thou, AUM, are the shrine of Brahman
    Robed in the cloak of Wisdom.
    Protect my learning,
    Happiness comes near and spreads over all.

This is a prayer for the attainment of wisdom and happiness
for one's offspring.

2. She quickly weaves
   Robes for herself,
   Cattle, provender,
   Refreshing purified water.
   So bring a happiness
   As wool does for sheep.
   Svaha![19]
   May the students of
   Brahman
   Come to hear me.
   Svaha!
   May they sit before one
   On all sides.
   May they practise restraint,
   May they enjoy peace.
   Svaha!

3. May I shine glory amongst the people,
   May I be superior to the rich,
   Which is not difficult,
   May I come unto you,
   Oh treasure, AUM.
   Svaha!
   Enter unto me, oh treasure.
   Svaha!
   In you consisting of a thousand branches
   I am cleansed as water flows downwards,

As the months progress in the year,
Oh divine protector of all worlds,
May Brahman students flock to me from all sides
Svaha!
Thou art a refuge,
Enlighten me,
Take hold of me,
Grasp me,
Seize me,
I am Thine.

Part 5

1. Bhu, this world,
   Bhuvas, the atmosphere,
   Suvas,[20] other worlds.
   These are the three
   Sacred affirmations.
   Maha Kamasya taught
   A fourth,
   Brahman
   Mahan,
   The Self of Consciousness,
   Reality, Love,
   The other three
   Are its members.

2. Mahan is also the Sun,
    All the worlds are
    Fostered by the Sun.
    Bhu is also Agni, fire,
    Bhuvas is Vayu, air,
    Suvas is Aditya, the Sun,
    Mahas is the gracious,
    Silvery crescent Moon
    Many heavenly lights
    Are fostered by the Moon.
    Bhu are the verses of the Rig Veda,
    Bhuvas are the verses of the Sama Veda,
    Suvas are the Yajur verses.

3. Mahas is Brahman,
    All Vedas are fostered by Brahman.
    Bhu is Prajna, the inhalation.
    Bhuvas is the exhalation.
    Suvas is Vyana, guttural breathing,
    Mahas is provender.
    All breathings and Pranayamas
    Are fostered by fresh food.
    So there are these permutations
    Of four times four,
    The four and four sacred invocations.
    He who understands these four
    Understands Brahman,
    All the Gods bring offerings to Brahman.

Part 6

1. There is ether in the Heart
And there dwells
The Supreme Spirit,
Consciousness,
Animating mind,
Immortal and golden.
Between the two
Upper and lower palates of the mouth
There hangs like a nipple the uvula,
The fleshy part of the upper palate;
That is the root of Indra,
From where he springs,
King of the Gods.
Also, where the root of the hair parts,
There Lord Indra opens the
Two sides of the head
And chanting Bhu
He enters as fire, Agni,
Bhuvas,
Chanting,
He enters as Vayu, air.

Hatha yoga has taught that placing the tongue on the upper palate turns off the inner dialogue of the continuous mind-brain's conceptual chattering. This verse also refers to the

chakra at the top of the skull. Many sages have experienced
the shakti energy (kundalini) rising up the spine, and heat
emerging from the top of the head. It is a yogic awakening and
was experienced by Ganapati Muni, Ramana Maharshi's main
disciple, according to his biographers.

2. Chanting Suvas
    He enters Aditya,
    The solar orb,
    Chanting Mahas
    He enters Brahman.
    He, exercising Lordship
    Over the mind-brain,
    Becomes Lord
    Of speech,
    Sight,
    Hearing,
    Knowledge.
    The body of this Brahman
    Is ethereal,
    Its nature is the True,
    Rejoicing in the senses,
    Delighted with the mind-brain,
    Perfect in peace,
    Immortal.
    Worship in this way
    Pracinayoga!

This is the mystical path of kundalini yoga and *must* only be practised under direction of a trusted teacher. It could be dangerous for the novice. Ramana Maharshi taught that these practices are not necessary for Self-Realization. Self-Enquiry and surrender were adequate means, and grace would bring about any changes needed automatically. It should never be forced. Deussen thinks Pracinayoga was probably the name of the pupil.

Part 7

1.   The Earth,
     Sky,
     Heaven,
     The Quarters,
     And their intermediates,
     Fire,
     Air,
     Sun,
     Moon,
     Stars,
     Water,
     Herbs,
     Trees,
     Ether,
     Universal Self,
     So much for mundane
     Objects.[21]

2.   With the body in the Self,
     There is inhalation,
     Exhalation,
     Guttural breathing,
     Onward breathing,
     The eye,
     Ear,
     Mind-brain,
     Speech,
     Touch,
     Skin,
     Flesh,
     Muscle,
     Bone,
     And marrow.
     Having contemplated on all
     These elemental arrangements
     Brought about by Consciousness,
     An Ancient Rishi
     Proclaimed the Truth:
     "Whatever exists is fivefold."

Part 8

1. AUM means Brahman,
   AUM means all,
   AUM means obedience.
   When the Brahmins are
   Cold
   They chant AUM.
   After AUM
   They sing Vedic Hymns,
   The ritual hymns,
   The responses,
   The Brahmin Priest gives instructions,
   The sacrificer permits
   The Vedic Fire Ceremony to proceed,
   When a Brahmin teaches
   He chants AUM.
   May I acquire the Veda
   As he does.

Part 9

1. What is needed?
   The right learning,
   Practising the Veda,
   Austerity,
   Restraint,

Tranquillity,
The Fires consecrated,
The Sacrifice performed,
Guests to be entertained,
Duty executed,
Marriage,
Bearing children,
Grandchildren.

2. All this and right learning,
    Practising the Veda,
    Rishi Rathitava advocates as Truth;
    Paurasishi recommends austerity;
    Mandgalya believes
    Learning and practising the Veda
    Are all that is needed,
    As this is both austerity and Truth.

Part 10

1. I am Brahman, he who shakes
    The tree mightily,
    The great awakener of the world tree,
    Which must be axed down by
    Discrimination and Self-Knowledge.

Brahman, as the Sat-Guru within the heart, speaks and shakes the tree of the world. Esoterically, illusion and egotism are axed to reveal knowledge of the Self as pure Consciousness. The poetry in this verse excels as it is by the famed poet Trisanku.

2. My glory shines like a high
   Snow-capped
   Mountain peak,
   In the Himalayan range.

3. I, whose pure light of
   Self-Knowledge
   Has ascended,
   I am "That",
   Truly Immortal,
   He that lives in the Sun
   Dwells in my Self.
   I am the brightest treasure,
   I am the embodiment
   Of Sage Wisdom,
   The projected core
   Of your inner being.
   This is the teaching of
   The poet Trisanku.

Part 11

1. After teaching the Veda
   The Sage
   Instructs the Pupil:
   "Say what is True,
   Do your duty!
   Never neglect study.
   After giving an offering
   To your Guru
   Do not cut off your children's support,
   Do not swerve from Truth or duty,
   Do not neglect what is of use or greatness,
   Never neglect the learning
   And teaching of the Veda.

2. Never neglect the sacrifice
   Due to Gods and Ancients.
   Let your Mother be to you
   As a Goddess,
   And your Father as a God,
   And your Teacher, a Guest.
   Actions which are blameless regarded
   As not done by others.
   Good deeds have been performed by us,
   Observe them too.

3/4.   There are Brahmins
Above us in understanding.
Comfort them, offer them a place,
Every Guru has his place,
Only give with faith,
Joy,
Modesty,
Respect,
Kindness.
If there is any doubt
Then consult your good judgement
And wise Brahmins.
Beware of over severity
Or negligence in duty.
So conduct yourself
This way,
This is the guide,
This is the Upanishadic thrust,
This is the ordainment,
This should be observed."

Part 12

1.   May Mitra the Sun
Be auspicious towards us
And Varuna, Aryaman
Indra and Brihaspati.

> May Vishnu take giant
> Strides towards us,
> Salutations to Brahman and Vayu,
> Thou art the perceptible Brahman.

These gods have been commented on in previous verses.

2. Of thou indeed have I spoken,
   I have spoken righteously,
   I have spoken truthfully.
   You have protected us all,
   Peace – peace – peace.

BOOK II

Hari Hi AUM,
May Brahman guard us,
Both Guru and Pupil.
May he enjoy us.
May we together acquire strength.
May our knowledge shine forth,
May we never dispute together,
Peace – peace – peace.

Part 1

He who understands Brahman
Knows the Supreme Brahman.
He who knows Brahman, the sole cause,
Which is Infinite Consciousness
Hidden in the depths of the Heart,
In the highest heavenly plane,
He enjoys all gifts at one
With all-seeing Brahman.
From "That" Self,
Brahman, Consciousness, Awareness,
Sprang air,
Through which we hear and breathe,
Fire,
Water,

Earth,
Herbs,
Food,
Seed,
Mankind.
Mankind is made of food essences.
There is the head,
Arms,
Body,
Spirit,
All for his support.

Part 2

From food come all earth-dwelling beings.
They live off food.
In the end they return as food.
Food is the "ancient panacea",
Herbs quieting heart and bodies.
They who worship food as Brahman
Receive food from Providence.
Different is the inner essence of the Inner Self
That depends on Life Breath or Prajna.
It follows the form of Man.
Life, the form of the Man,
Is the form of the Self.
Inhalation is its head,

Guttural breathing is its right arm,
Exhalation is its left arm,
Ether, the trunk,
Earth the base.

Universal archetypal man is created in the divine image, the Self is described analogously.

Part 3

The Gods breathe from Life Breath
So do men, women and cattle.
Breath is the life of all beings
Therefore it is all enlivening.
They who worship Life Breath as Brahman
Obtain the fulfilment of Life.
The embodied Self depending on breath
Is the same as that which depends
On the essence of foods.
But the Inner Self is different
As mind is involved.
It too has the form of mankind.
The Yajur Veda is its head,
The Rig Veda its right arm,
The Sama Veda its left arm.
The teaching of the Brahmins
Its body,

The Atharva Veda Hymns are
Its support.

The knowledge of the Vedas is the correct content of the mind
in this aristocratic, higher, ancient culture and civilization.

Part 4

He who knows only the love of Brahman,
From whom all speech flows,
With the power of reason only
Fails to reach "That".[22]
Yet he never fears,
The embodiment of this mind
From the Self
Is the same as embodiment
Of Brahmanic love from
The Life Force.
The Inner Self which
Is made up of "understanding"
Differs from the intellectual make-up.
It follows the form of mankind.[23]
Faith forms the head,
Righteousness is the right arm,
The Truth is the left arm,
Absorption in Yoga is its body,
The subtle intellect is the support.

Part 5

Understanding carries out the sacrifice
And performs all sacred rites.
All Gods worship understanding as Brahman,
The Primeval, Ancient One.
If man knows understanding as Brahman,
And if he does not swerve away,
He leaves all suffering behind in the body
And fulfils his wishes.
The embodied Self of understanding
Is the same as the mind,
Different is the Inner Self,
Made up of Love.
It also follows the form of mankind.
Joy is its head,
Satisfaction is the right arm,
Fulfilment is the left arm,
Bliss the body,
Brahman the support.

Part 6

He who knows the Brahman
As No Thing
Becomes No Thing also.
He who thinks Brahman is an entity,

Him we see also as an entity.
The embodied Self of this love
Is the same as understanding.
The Pupil now enquires:
"Do they who do not know this travel
To the world of Brahman after death?
Or must they wait to know 'That' after death?"
The Sage answers:
"Brahman at rest
Wished
To create.
He wished to be many,
To grow forth,
To enjoy his own exuberance and play,
To know himself in manifestation.
He brooded
Like a hen on her eggs
Or like a Rishi performing austerities,
After hatching, he impelled the All, 'what is'
Simply to be.
Having created,
He entered into his creation,
He became Sat,
What is manifestly Real,
And Asat,
Unmanifest,
Defined,

Undefined,
Supported,
Unsupported,
Knowledgeable,
Not knowing,
Like stones,
Real
And
Unreal
At the same time.
'The True' became all 'That'
The wise call 'That' Brahman *The True*.

Objects can be real and unreal at the same time. For example, at the level of empiric life a stone appears to be "real". At the level of quantum physics it is an energy field obeying certain laws for a time. It is largely space, electrons, atoms, etc., without any reality except in the consciousness of the observer.

Part 7

In the beginning
That was non-existence,
Only potential energy at rest,
Unmanifest,
Formless, nameless,

From 'That'
Emerged
'What Is'.
'That' made itself its Self,
It was Self-Created.
That which is Self-Created
Was a flavour,
A taste and look of beauty.
After perceiving beauty
One can experience pleasure.
Who would breathe, exhales.
In that Love dwells Brahman.
It did not exist in only the
Ether of the Heart centre
Within another centre.
He alone causes Grace.
When the devotee finds
Freedom from fear,
Rest and trust in 'That' Power
Which knows the way
To Self-Realization,
Invisible,
Bodiless,
Undefined,
Unsupported,
Then he has touched Brahman
The Courageous.

If he makes small, petty, intellectual,
Nit-picking
Distinctions about Brahman
Fear will spring out and sting him
Like a scorpion.
That fear exists only for those
Who think they are clever,
Like pundits and scholars,
Not for the Sage."

These answers of the teacher are a deeply profound philosophic poem. Ramesh Balsekar has also written a profound creation poem echoing the earlier part of this creation hymn as an appendix to his early book, *Pointers*. See my *Wisdom of Ramesh Balsekar* (Watkins, 2003).

Part 8

This section is on bliss or *ananda*:

From fear of Brahman
The wind howls
Like a banshee,
Suns awake from slumber
Like young lions,
Fire leaps
Like gazelles in chase,

The Gods quake
Like jellies,
And Death flees
Like a coward in battle.
Now I will tell you about
Blissful love,
The Queen Ananda.
Let us imagine a noble youth,
Handsome,
Well versed in the Veda,
Intelligent,
Quick,
Alert,
Firm,
Brave,
Strong,
Diligent,
Wealthy,
That is one measure of
Blissful love
Bestowed on him.
Multiply this one hundred times,
This is a drop of
Blissful love
Felt by the Saints and Sages
Wise in Advaita Vedanta,
Now free from desires.

Multiply "That" one hundred
Times more,
Then the blissful love of Saints
Is a mere drop of the bliss of
Celestial Angels,[24]
And likewise of a Mahatma[25]
Free from desires.
One hundred times that blissful love
Of Celestial Angels
Is one drop
Of the Primeval,
Primordial
Ancient One,
Enjoying Eternity,
Like a Great Jnani
Teaching by Silence,[26]
Free from desires.
One hundred times
The blissful love of the Ancient Ones
Is one drop of "That"
Of a body
Born in heaven
Through merit
And like
A Maharshi[27]
Free from desires.
One hundred times

The blissful love of the Gods
Conceived in heaven,
Is one drop
Of the bliss of the Gods of Sacrifice
Who visit other Gods
By means of Vedic Sacrifice,
Like a Bhagavan[28] born on Earth
Free from desires.
One hundred times the
Bliss of the thirty-three Deities
Is one drop
Of the blissful love of Indra,
King of the Gods,
And like a Primeval Sage[29]
Who teaches by Silence
Free from desires.
One hundred times the bliss
Of Indra
Is one drop of the blissful
Love
Of Brihaspati,[30]
Like a Self-Realized liberated Being
Free from desires.
One hundred times the bliss of
Brihaspati
Is one drop of the blissful
Love of Prajapati,[31]

Like a Jivan-Mukta
Free from desires.
One hundred times the bliss of
Prajapati is one drop of the
Blissful love of Brahman,
Like the Supreme Sage
Dakshinamurti.
He who is "That" Brahman
In man or woman
And he who is "That" Brahman in the Sun
Are One.
He who comprehends all "That"
When he leaves the body
Reaches the Self,
Consisting of subtle food essence,
Life Breath,
Subtle Intellect,
Understanding,
And Love – Bliss – Ananda.

Part 9

He who knows the Love-Bliss
Of "That" Brahman
From whom all speech flows,
Turns away unable to reach "That".
He fears nothing.

He or she does not disturb himself or herself
With the thought,
"Why did I not perform only good?
Why did I do some bad?"
He who truly sees the
Relativity of the polar opposites,
Good and bad,
And that all actions are God's,
Is liberated.
This is the Upanishad.

This verse essentially contains the *para vidya* or higher knowledge.

BOOK III

Hari Hi AUM.
May Brahman guard us,
May he enjoy us,
May we gain strength through him,
May our knowledge shine forth,
May we never dispute with one another,
Peace – peace – peace.

Part 1

Bhrigu went to his
Father, the God Varuna,
Asking to be taught about Brahman.
Varuna replied:
"Food,
Breath,
Eye,
Ear,
Mind,
Speech,
'That' from whence all beings are born,
'That' by which, when born, they live,
'That' into which they enter at death
'That' is Brahman."
He performed severe austerities.

Part 2

He saw food to be Brahman,
For from food essences beings emerge.
They live by food and become food at death.
Having seen this he went again to his Father,
Asking to be taught Brahman.
Varuna answered:
"Try to know Brahman through
Performing austerities,
This is a means to know Brahman."

Part 3

He then saw that breath is Brahman,
For by breath beings are conceived,
By breath when born they live,
Into breath they return at death.
Having seen this, he again
Asked his Father to teach him Brahman.
Again Varuna advised austerities
As a way to learn.

Part 4

He saw that mind is Brahman,
For out of mind beings are born,
Through mind, when born, they live,
Back into the Source as Consciousness,
The Great Mind, they return at death.
Having seen this, he asked
His Father again to teach him Brahman.
Again Varuna advised
Austerities as a means to learn.

Part 5

Bhrigu then saw that
Understanding was Brahman,
Out of understanding beings are born,
Through understanding when born they live.
At death they return to the
Ultimate Understanding.
Having seen this he again
Went to Varuna to learn more.
Varuna again advised him
To practise austerities as a means to knowledge.

Part 6

Bhrigu saw that bliss-full love was Brahman,
Out of bliss-full love beings are conceived
From bliss-full love they are born and they live.
At death they return to the Source of bliss-full
Love, Ananda.
This is the Brahman Knowledge
Of Bhrigu and Varuna exalted
In the highest heaven and in the Heart.
He who knows "That" becomes
Similarly exalted,
Becomes provided with healthy food
And is able to enjoy it,
Is blest by worthy offspring and cattle,
And by the splendour of
His Brahman Knowledge
He becomes well known.

Part 7

A rule is never to abuse
Food through waste or staleness.
Breath is also a food
The body enjoys it.
The body needs breath,
Breath depends on a body.

So food depends on food.
He who knows this rests exalted,
Is provided with healthy fresh food,
Is magnified by children, many cattle
And the great splendour of his
Brahman Knowledge.

Healthy food is fresh "sattvic" food based on a vegetarian diet – pulses, grains, vegetables, fruit and milk products. This was the regime advocated by Ramana Maharshi as a great aid to Self-Realization; to develop a sattvic mind.

Part 8

Let him never refuse
Nourishing food,
This is a rule!
Water is food,
Even light needs its food.
So food depends on food.
He who knows this rests exalted,
Becomes well provided
For with fresh food
And a healthy appetite,
He becomes great through children, cattle
And the fame of his Brahmanic Knowledge.

The Upanishad seems to warn against fasting as a means of spiritual growth. Starving the body is a sin. The middle way between asceticism and indulgence is the golden mean, taught by the Buddha and other sages. We are in touch with a higher knowledge beyond the intellect in these Upanishads.

Part 9

Let him or her harvest much food,
That is a rule.
Earth is food for the Ethereal.
The Ethereal needs the Earth,
The Earth depends on the Ethereal.
This is food depending on food.
He who understands this becomes exalted.
Rich in good food
With a healthy appetite,
He becomes magnified by
Children and children's children, many cattle
And the fame of his splendid
Brahmanic Knowledge.

Part 10

1. Never turn away the stranger
   From one's house,
   This is a rule.
   Thereby a man will
   Acquire much food
   To give to worthy people.
   Tell the stranger:
   "There is food ready for you."
   If he gives food generously
   He receives ample food in return.
   If he gives food equally,
   Food is given to him equally in return.
   If, however, he gives food stingily
   Then food is given to him stingily in return.

This is the secret of Indian hospitality to guests, mendicants, and strangers. Many sages have begged for food following this injunction.

2. He who understands "That"
   Recognizes and so worships
   Brahman in the other
   As the ability to speak,
   Inhale,
   Exhale,

To exercise,
Skill with hands,
Walk with feet,
And excrete.
These are human recognitions
Of Brahman in action.
Now follow the recognitions of Brahman
With reference to the Gods,
As joy in rainfall,
As power in the lightning flash.

3. As there is glory in cattle,
    Shining bright lights in the stars,
    As joy in the act of procreation,
    As in the fact of Immortality,
    And in the blissful phallic member,[32]
    As everything Ethereal.
    Worship "That Brahman" as support
    And he becomes supported.
    Worship Brahman
    As greatness and become great.
    Worship Brahman as intelligence,
    And become intelligent.

4. Worship "That Brahman" as love
   And all petty desires
   Bow down before him, as love.
   Let him simply worship Brahman as Brahman
   And transcend language.
   He will then become the Brahman
   Of Consciousness, Awareness, Peace, Self, Love.
   "That" he already is
   But fails to recognize it, alas!
   And suffers unnecessarily.
   Let him worship "That"
   As the "Samadhi" of the Gods in Brahman
   His enemies who hate him will perish all around
   All around him will die, his inner foes[33] too.
   They will fall off as leaves
   Of oak trees in Autumn.
   He who is "That Brahman" in mankind
   And "That" which is in the Sun are One,
   The same.

5. He who understands "That"
   When he has left the body
   After reaching and knowing the Self
   Of Consciousness, Reality, Love,
   Made of foods,
   Breath,
   Mind,

Understanding,
Bliss,
Enters and enjoys these worlds,
Being provided with ample foods,
Assuming any form he likes,
He sits and sings
The Hymns of Brahman,
Bhavu, Bhavu, Bhavu,
Oh wonderful, oh wonderful,
Oh wonderful, indeed!

6. I am food!
I am food to be eaten,
I am the eater of food,
I am the poet who links
The two as One,
I am the first born
Of the righteous harmony.
Before the Gods
I was in the centre
Of all "That" which is Immortal.
He who sacrifices me,
He alone preserves me.
He who eats food
I too eat, as food.
I overcome the whole world,
I am endowed with

Golden light
Like the blazing Sun.
He who knows "That"
Reaches "That"
This is the Secret Tradition.[34]
This is the Upanishad.

To be eaten by the gods as food and to eat food is man's privilege. Shiva was the cook who devoured egos, esoterically.

THE AITAREYA UPANISHAD

Introduction

This Upanishad belongs to the Rig Veda. It aims to lead the performer of sacrificial ceremonies away from the exoteric outer meaning to the inner esoteric understanding, from the *apara vidya* to the *para vidya*. Shankara writes about three different types of men and women. The highest are those who have turned away from worldly values, are self-collected, and eager for liberation. For these II: 4–6 is meant. There are others who wish to reach liberation more gradually. For them II: 1–3 is meant. There are those still worried about worldly possessions. For them Book III[35] is meant. I have extended the transcreation to the beginning of Book II, Part 6, including more than most popular abridgements. The first book is largely a description of the Mahavrata ceremony. Most traditionally this is omitted from the Upanishad, which properly begins with Book II.

BOOK II

Part 1

1. This is the way,
   This sacrifice
   And "That" Brahman
   This is the Truth.

2. Let no man or woman
   Swerve from it,
   Let no man or woman
   Transgress it.

3. The Ancient Rishis
   Never transgressed.
   Those that died through ignorance
   Became bewildered.

4. This has been uttered
   By a Great Rishi[36]
   Three types of people
   Transgressed.
   Others settled down around
   The ancient Agni Fire,
   The magnificent Sun
   Shone in the midst of the worlds,

Vayu, the air,
Entered the dawns
At the ends of the Earth.

5. The three classes
Who transgressed
Are what we see as
Earth, birds, trees,
Herbs and reptiles.

The *apara vidya* (exoteric conventional religious teaching)
uses these injunctions to ensure people do not stray from
righteous harmony. Morality was upheld in ancient India for
thousands of years through this and similar beliefs. Police
only became necessary under British rule in the 19th century.

6. Those who settled down
Were those who sat
To worship Agni, the fire.

7. The great who stood
In the midst
Of the world
Is Aditya, the Sun,
Radiant,
Resplendent,
Shining,

Blazing,
Brilliant,
Effulgent.

8. The winds entered the dawns
    Meaning that Vayu, air,
    The great purifier
    Entered every corner of the Earth,
    Cleansing, and purifying as the rain
    Cleans the world from its dust.

Part 2

1. People call for hymns,
    Without understanding the
    Significance of a hymn.
    The Hymn is "That" from
    Which the favour of the Gods arises
    As the Earth,
    From all whatsoever that exists,
    Arises.

To glorify the creation is in itself a poem – a hymn of devotion
for the gods, not merely a song of praise.

2. The object of the Hymn
   Is Agni, fire,
   The eighty verses are its
   Succour,
   For by means of succour
   All is known.

Agni represents the intermediary, vicar, or mediator between mankind and the divine. The fire is Promethean, a gift from the gods or grace. Sri Aurobindo has written a brilliant essay in his introduction to the *Hymns of Agni*, entitled "Hymns of Mystic Fire", stressing the significance of Agni.

3. The Great Hymn is Creation
   Set in the sapphire sky,
   Wherein colourful birds chirp and fly,
   And mankind marches on resolutely.
   The object of this praise is Vayu, air,
   The eighty verses are succour,
   For by their means all is known.

4. The Great Hymn is truly a heaven,
   For from its gift of rainfall
   All that exists on Earth arises.
   The object of her praise
   Is Aditya, the Sun.

    The eighty verses are succour
    For by "That" one reaches the all.

5.   So much for the Gods,
    Now for mankind.

6.   The Great Hymn is truly mankind,
    He and she are great,
    They are Prajapati,
    Lord of Creation,
    Let us meditate,
    I am That Hymn.

7.   The Hymn is in his mouth
    As it is in the Earth.

8.   He praises speech,
    The eighty verses
    Are succour,
    By means of which he knows
    All and everything.

9.   For mankind
    The Hymn is in the nostrils,
    Microcosm of the sky.

10. The Hymn praises breath,
    The eighty verses
    Are succour[37]
    For by means of "That"
    He obtains all and everything.

11. The root of the nostril
    Is, as it were, the place of heaven.

This is a mysterious verse and shows that the rishis with their explorative intelligence discovered sacred places the modern mind has not cognized. Attention on the root of the nostril may reveal the meaning of this verse?

12. This Hymn is the fore brow
    Between the eyes,
    A resemblance of heaven.
    It praises the eye.
    The eighty verses are succour
    By which means he reaches
    All and everything.

These verses are very mystical and may only be understood by placing the attention on where the Upanishad indicates, the chakra between the brows, or pineal gland, a favourite resting place in meditation, as is the right side of the chest.

13. The eighty verses of the Great Hymn
    Are succour
    To the Gods and mankind.
    All these beings have to breathe
    And eat substance as food.
    But by succour, given with love,
    He conquers the world
    And by succour given in sacrifice
    He conquers other worlds unknown
    To him and human knowledge.
    So the eighty verses are
    Succour to the Gods and mankind.

14. All this is
    "That" succour
    And all that consumes succour is the Earth
    For from the Earth arises
    "What is" – here and now,
    The only moment –
    The present Eternal Now.

15. All that dies on Earth,
    Heaven consumes,
    And all that returns there
    Is transmigrated
    Into a new life
    To serve the Divine Will,[38]

The Earth, in time, consumes all,
Including the Jnani, sage.

16. The Earth is therefore
Provider and consumer,
Consumer and consumed.
No one owns that which
He does not consume
Or does not consume him.

Part 3

1. We shall trace the
Origin of seed,
The seed of Prajapati,
Lord of Creatures, are the Gods.
The seed of the Gods is rain.
The seed of rain are herbs.
That of herbs is food,
The seed of food is seed,
The seed of seed are creatures,
The seed of creatures,
Is the Heart.[39]
The seed of the Heart is mind.
The seed of mind is speech.
The seed of speech is action.
Action done in a former state is this mankind,
The dwelling place of Brahman.

2.   Man is made of food
     And because he is made of food
     Gold is inherent in him.
     He who sees this becomes golden.
     In the planes of being to come
     He or she is seen to be golden as the Sun
     For the benefit of all beings.

This verse is a word play on *iramaya*, "made of food", and
hwanmaya, "made of gold".

Part 4

1.   Brahman is the form
     Of sacred Prajna,
     The Life Breath,
     Which entered into mankind
     From the tips of his toes.
     So the tips of the toes
     Are called prapada,
     Like hoof and claws in animals.

2.   Then Brahman as Prajna
     Permeated higher
     Into the thighs.

3. Then he uttered
   "Grasp wide"
   And entered the belly.

4. Then he called
   "Make room"
   And entered the chest.

5. Some meditate on
   The belly as Brahman,[40]
   Others on the head.
   Both are Brahman.

6. Now Brahman crept up
   And entered the head.

7. Then the delights of
   Sight, hearing, mind, speech,
   And breath arose.

8. Delights alight on he or she
   Who understands why
   The head is so informed.

9. These senses
   Strove together
   Chanting
   "I Am the Hymn."

On leaving his or her body
We shall depart
And he or she shall
Be the Hymn amongst us.

10. Speech began without speaking,
Men and women ate and drank.
Sight began without seeing,
The same began with hearing,
Thinking and breathing.

11. The body was decaying
All the time
And was so called mortal.

12. If a man or woman knows this,
Then his or her wicked enemy
Who hates them is defeated.

13. They strove again
Chanting,
"I Am the Hymn."
They decided to re-enter
The body.
The body will rise again
He or she shall be the Hymn
Amongst us.

14. Speech,
    Sight,
    Mind,
    Entered,
    But the body lay still,
    But when breath entered
    The body arose
    And treasured the Hymn.

15. So breath alone is the Hymn

16. Let all people know
    "That".

17. The other senses spoke
    To the breath:
    "You are the Hymn,
    You are all 'That',
    We are yours, you are ours."

18. A Great Rishi
    Proclaimed,
    "You are ours, we are yours."[41]

Part 5

1. Then the Gods carried
    The Life Breath forward,
    The Life Breath was extended,
    It was morning.
    When the Life Breath rested
    It was evening.
    Day is therefore its inhalation,
    Night its exhalation.

2. Speech is fire, Agni,
    Sight the Sun, Aditya,
    Mind the Moon.
    Nearing the four quarters
    There is the Union of these Gods,
    So they dwell in the body
    And also amongst the Gods.

3. Hiranyadal Vaida
    Who knew "That"
    And by his knowledge
    Had become Universal Spirit,
    Said: "Whatever they do not give to me
    They do not own themselves.
    I know the Union
    Of the Gods in the body,
    This is 'That'."

4. To he or she who knows
   "That",
   All creatures, freely, offer
   Gifts.

5. That breath is Sattya,
   The True.
   Sat is breath,
   Ti is food,
   Yam is the Sun.
   This is triple,
   Triple too is the eye
   Being white, dark,
   And pupil.
   He who knows why
   True is True,
   Even if he appears to speak
   Falsely,
   What he says is True.

Part 6

1. Speech is the rope of
   Breath,
   The names
   Its knots.
   By this all is bound.

    All have names
And speech ties them neatly up together.

Most translators end the Aitareya with different verses to its repetitive conclusion. This verse is a strong metaphor on which to close.

THE MUNDAKA UPANISHAD

This profound Upanishad comes from the Atharva Veda. *Mund* means "to shave". He who understands this Upanishad is "shaved" from ignorance. The Upanishad clearly makes the distinction between the *para vidya*, the higher teaching of the Supreme Brahman and the *apara vidya*, the lower teaching of the world of appearance. It is by this understanding one reaches Brahmanic knowledge.

BOOK I

Part 1

1. Brahma was first of the Gods,
   Creator of the Universe,
   Preserver of the World.
   He taught the knowledge of Brahman
   To his eldest son Atharvan.

2. What Brahma taught to him,
   He taught Angir,
   Who taught Bharadraga,
   Who taught Angirin.

3. Saunaka, a Great Householder,
   Asked Angirin the question:
   "What is 'That' through which
   If it is known, all else is known?"

4. Angirin replied:
   "Two types of knowledge
   Must be clearly understood,
   The higher knowledge
   Or Para Vidya,
   The lower knowledge
   Or Apara Vidya.

This is a principle underlying all Hindu scripture, emphasized by Shankara and the expositions of sages. Concessions are made for the people with lower knowledge. Only the intellectually evolved can understand the higher teaching. Briefly stated the *apara vidya* is the exoteric knowledge for the ordinary man or woman; the *para vidya* or higher teaching (Advaita Vedanta) was reserved for the Brahmin. Nowadays it is available to earnest seekers, even Westerners, without a Hindu background. Such is divine grace. Ramana Maharshi, Ramakrishna and Ramesh Balsekar have made this open secret available to all who are receptive.

5. The lower knowledge
   Are the Four Vedas:
   Phonetics,
   Ceremonies,
   Grammar,
   Etymology,
   Meter,
   Astronomy.
   The higher knowledge
   Is the direct apperception
   Of the Indestructible Brahman,
   The Self,
   Consciousness, Reality, Love,
   Peace, beyond words.

6. 'That' which is invisible,
   Ungraspable,
   Without family,
   Cattle,
   Bodily form,
   The Eternal,
   Omnipresent,
   All pervading
   Imperishable
   Consciousness,
   'That' is which the sages

Know
As the Source of all Being,
Consciousness, Reality, Love.

7. As the spider
    Spins
    And draws in its web,
    As plants grow,
    As hair springs from the head and body,
    So does all
    Arise from this Indestructible Consciousness.

8. Brahman increases by way
    Of a brooding
    So issues forth all matter,
    Breath,
    Mind,
    Truth,
    Words,
    Deeds,
    Immortality.

9. From he or she who sees all,
    Who knows all,
    Whose brooding and pondering
    Consists of knowledge
    From the Supreme Brahman,

Is born the Brahman
The Hiranyagarbha
Of name, form and matter.

Part 2

1. This the lower knowledge,
   The Apara Vidya,
   The sacrificial ceremonies
   The Poets saw in the Vedic Hymns
   Were performed
   In the Silver Age.[42]
   Practise them punctiliously
   You devotees,
   This is the path that leads
   To heaven through good deeds.

2. When the fire is lit
   The flame flickers,
   Let men and women
   Make offerings into ghee[43]
   With Great Faith.

3. If a man's Fire Sacrifice
   Is not followed by the lunar quarterly
   And at harvest times,
   Or is unattended by guests,

Or not offered at all,
Unceremoniously,
Then he destroys the seven worlds.

4.   Kali, blackest black,
Karah, fearsomely terrific,
Manogara, swift as thought,
Suloheta, brilliant red,
Sudhumvavarna, deep purple,
Sphulingini, sparkling light,
Visvarupi, possessing all forms brilliantly,
These are the seven tongues
Of the Sacred Fire.

5.   If a man or woman
Performs sacred ceremonies
While these flames are flickering,
At the right time,
Then as sure as the rays of the Sun
They will lead him or her to heaven
Where Indra lives.

6.   Come here, come here,
The brilliant offerings call,
And carry the sacrifices
On solar beams
While they chant praises

Saying: 'This is the heavenly world
Gained by good works.'

From the Advaitic standpoint (those who follow the *para
vidya*) these promises of heaven for good deeds (*apara vidya*)
reinforce the divine hypnosis. The Advaitin sees all as the will
of Brahman and all as Consciousness. Ramana Maharshi,
Nisargadatta Maharaj and Ramesh Balsekar exemplify this
teaching for our age. See my books: *The Wisdom of Ramesh
Balsekar* (Watkins Publishing, 2003); *The Bhagavad Gita –
A Transcreation* (O Books, John Hunt Publishing, 2003);
and *Shankara, Ramana and The Forty Verses* (Watkins
Publishing, 2002).

7. Fragile
   Are the rafts,
   The eighteen sacrifices
   Of the lower ceremonial.
   Those who claim this
   Is the highest teaching
   Are fools
   And will remain so until
   Senility and death.

8. Fools live in darkness,
   Wise in their own conceit,
   Puffed up with vain concepts.

They go round and round
As on a treadmill
Like blind led by the blind,[44]
Or dogs chasing their own tails.

9. Children who have
Lived in ignorance
For a long time
Imagine they are happy,
But in remorseless time,
Those who rely on their goods,
Owing to powerful
Passions,
Fall headlong,
Feel wretched,
When they approach death.

10. Believing sacrifices and
Good deeds
As the best,
These fools see no
Higher good
And having enjoyed their reward
In a mind-projected heaven,
They transmigrate into
Another body here,
Or in a lower world.

This verse is a good example of the *apara vidya*, dismissing there may be reincarnation into an imaginary heaven. The belief in reincarnation is however socially useful in ensuring good behavior amongst the masses. Transmigration of the subtle body back to Consciousness as the source to be utilized for more lives is a higher teaching. It explains child prodigies who can compose music at five, like Mozart.

11. But those who practise
    Austerity
    And hold Great Faith,
    Who retire into the forest
    Calm,
    Wise,
    Living on gifts,
    Leave the body
    Free from passion,
    Through the Sun
    To the perceptible Brahman.

This verse refers to the rishis and true renunciates who gave the revelation of the higher teaching of the Upanishads to mankind.

12. Let a lover of Brahman,
     After he has examined
     All worth
     Gained as a reward
     For deeds,
     Gain, also, freedom
     From compelling desires.
     Nothing Eternal can be
     Gained by what is
     Not eternally made.
     Let him or her in order
     To understand 'That'
     Find a true guru,
     Who is wise
     And gives him peace
     Dwelling totally in Brahman.

Beware of the false gurus who exploit their disciples and claim enlightenment. The true guru never claims enlightenment, for that which says "I am enlightened" is the egotistic obstacle to enlightenment. The true guru is implicitly enlightened, others revere him and feel peace in his presence. Many have been, and are being enlightened through the resonance that takes place between the true guru and pupil, external or in the heart.

13.   To that devotee
     Who approaches with respect,
     Who is thought to be free
     From desires,
     Who is at peace,
     The Sage truly tells
     The knowledge of Brahman
     As Consciousness, Reality, Love, Self,
     Through which he or she too will
     Also know 'That' as well.

BOOK II

Part 1

1. This is the Truth,
   As from a blazing fire,
   Sparks[45] fly up
   A thousandfold,
   So are different beings
   Created by the Eternal Source,
   And return there too.

2. The Creative Source
   Is bodiless,
   He is without and within,
   Unborn,
   Without the need of breath,
   Mind, pure,
   Higher than the High Imperishable.

3. From Brahman,
   When Creation begins,
   Brain,
   Mind,
   Sense organs,
   Air,
   Light,

Water,
Earth,
Are born.
He is the support of all.

4. Fire, the sky is head,
    Sun and Moon, eyes,
    Corners of space, ears,
    Vedas, revealed speech.
    Wind, breath,
    Heart, universe,
    From feet came Earth,
    'That' is indeed the inner Self,
    Consciousness,
    Ruler of all.

5. From 'That' comes
    Agni, fire,
    The Sun, fuel
    The Moon sends rain,
    The Earth, herbs,
    Plants, seed in his wife,
    Many beings are born
    From the Supreme Being
    In the Heart.

6.   From him comes
     The Vedas,
     The sacrifices,
     The rewards to priests,
     The year,
     The sacrifices,
     The other worlds
     Where the Moon
     Shines as brightly
     As the Sun.

7.   From him
     Come the Gods,
     The Genii,
     Mankind,
     Herds,
     Birds,
     Inhalation,
     Exhalation,
     Rice and corn
     For sacrifices,
     Austerity,
     Faith,
     Truth,
     Restraint,
     Law,
     Dharma,
     The Righteous Way.

8. The seven senses,
   The seven lights,
   Acts of sensation,
   The seven fuels
   By which the senses
   Are illuminated,
   The seven sacrifices,
   The seven worlds
   Where the senses move,
   Which rest in the Heart-cave,
   Placed there seven times seven.

9. From these come the seas,
   All the many mountains,
   The rivers, herbs,
   And the juice by which
   The inner Self subsists
   Along with the elements.

10. The Supreme Being
    In all 'That',
    Sacrifice,
    Penance,
    Brahman,
    The Highest Eternal,
    He who knows 'That'
    Hidden in the Heart-cave,

He or she, oh friend,
Shatters the fetters of ignorance on Earth.

Part 2

1. Manifest, near,
   Moving, in the Heart-cave,
   Closer than your own breathing,
   Is the Supreme Being,
   In 'That' all is centred,
   Which you know
   As moving,
   Breathing,
   Bringing,
   Blinking,
   Being and not-being
   As Beloved,
   The Best,
   Beyond all creatures' understanding.

2. That which is brilliant,
   Smaller than the smallest,
   On which all worlds are based
   And the beings who live there,
   'That' is the indestructible Brahman,
   Consciousness, Reality, Love,
   The Breath,

Speech,
Mind,
The True,
The Eternal,
This is the target to be struck
With the sharp arrow of attention,
Strike it friends!

3. Lift up these Upanishads
As your mighty bow,
As the great weapon,
Place on it an arrow
Well honed by devotion!
Then draw hard on the strings
With an aim directed.
Let go to 'That', 'What is',
Strike the mark,
Realize, recognize,
Oh friend,
That which is imperishable in you
And envelopes you,
Consciousness, Awareness, Peace,
Love, Source, God,
Sat-Chit-Ananda.

4. AUM is that bow,
    The Self
    Of Consciousness, Reality,
    Love is the arrow,
    Atman-Brahman its aim.
    It is to be loosed by a man or woman
    Who is intelligent,
    Then the arrow becomes one
    With the target,
    He or she becomes one
    With Atman-Brahman.

5. In he or she,
    Heaven,
    Earth,
    Sky
    Are interwoven
    As a great tapestry
    By the mind,
    By the senses.
    Know 'That' alone as
    The Self of Consciousness
    And forget other words
    And concepts!
    'That' is the bridge to the Eternal.

6. He moves,
   Resting in the Heart
   Where arteries meet,
   Like spokes in a wheel
   Fastened firmly to its nave.
   Meditate on the Self
   Of Consciousness, Reality, Love,
   As AUM,
   Victory to you, dear friend,
   That you may cross
   To the other shore
   Beyond the sea of ignorance.

7. He or she who understands the All,
   Who knows All,
   He or she to whom All
   This Glory belongs,
   The Self is ethereal.
   In the heavenly city of
   Brahman in the Heart,
   He or she discerns
   The nature of the mind
   And guides the body and senses.
   He or she subsists in food essences
   Close to the Heart.
   He or she who understands 'That'
   Beholds the Eternal
   Who shines forth full of Love.

8. The iron fetters that
Bind the Heart
Are shattered
By the axe of discrimination,
All doubts are resolved,
Deeds and their effects die
When he or she sees through
The laws of cause and effect.[46]

9. In the Supreme Golden Sheath
Rests Brahman,
Free from passions,
Indivisible,
'That' is pure,
Light of lights,
The Self of Self-Knowledge,
Consciousness, Reality, Love.

10. The Sun does not shine there,
Nor the Moon, the stars,
The lightning flash,
Nor does fire blaze.
When Brahman shines
The All shines by 'That'
By this light all is lit.

11.   That Eternal Brahman
       Is before, behind,
       Right, left,
       Above, below.
       'That' alone is
       All this, 'What is', is sheer perfection.

This verse echoes the opening of the Isa Upanishad.

BOOK III

Part 1

1. Two beautiful parrots,
   Multicoloured with exotic plumes,
   Who were inseparable friends,
   Perched on the same tree.
   One of them eats sweet berries,
   The other watches silently not eating.

2. On the same Tree of Life
   One man is suffering,
   Identified,
   Confused by his own
   Powerlessness.
   But when he glimpses the
   Other Lord,
   His own Consciousness, Awareness,
   Self,
   Contented,
   He knows his glory
   And suffering vanishes.

3. When the seer then glimpses
   The brilliant Creator,
   Lord of the Universe
   As this same Consciousness,

Who has his Source in Brahman
Also 'That' Consciousness,
He is wise,
Transcending the dualities
Of good and evil
He touches Unity,
Free from desires.

4. Brahman
Is the breath
Animating all beings.
Understanding 'That'
Is wisdom.
He ceases from merely talking.
He revels in Love
And Consciousness, Awareness,
Of his own Self.
He delights in 'That',
And having performed the
Sacred acts
Of Truthfulness,
Restraint
And meditation on 'What Is',
Brahman,
He rests in the Heart
Firmly established in Brahman,
The Self.

He is the best of those who
Know 'That'.

5. By truthfulness,
   By restraint,
   Right knowledge,
   Austerity,
   The recognition of one's own
   Self as Consciousness,
   Awareness and Love
   Is gained,
   'That' which pure
   Forest sages know
   Is like a light within the body.

6. Truth prevails by 'That',
   The path is laid,
   The way of the Gods
   By which the Ancient Rishis,
   Fully satisfied,
   Proceed to the Highest Plane of Truth.

7. 'That', True Brahman
   Shines forth magnificently,
   Divine,
   Inconceivable,
   Smaller than the smallest.

Beyond what is far yet near,
Hidden in the Heart-cave,
Among those who know 'That'
For ever more.

8. Neither the eye,
   Speech nor senses
   Apprehend 'That',
   Nor by austerity
   Or good works
   Is 'That' reached.
   When a man or woman's nature
   Is purified by the calm clear light
   Of Advaita Knowledge,
   Then they enjoy
   Meditating on 'That'
   As Indivisible.

9. That subtle Self of Consciousness
   Is to be understood by
   Apperception,
   When the breath has entered
   Fivefold,
   For every thought of man
   And woman is interwoven
   With the senses.
   When thought is clarified,

Then knowledge of the Self
As Consciousness arises.

10.   Whatever state
A man or woman
Whose understanding is clarified
Imagines,
Whatever he wishes for himself
Or herself or for others,
That state he conquers,
Those wishes are granted.
So let every man or woman
Who wishes happiness
Honour the man or woman
Who realizes the Self
As Consciousness, Awareness, Love,
Sat-Chit-Ananda.

Part 2

1.   He or she, knower of the Self,
Reaches 'That' highest plane of Brahman
In which all is contained
And shines brightly.
The wise, who without craving happiness
Worship 'That' Supreme Knower of the Self
Transcend this seedbed of transmigration.

2. He who forms mental desires
   Is transmigrated
   Through his wishes ever here and there.
   ⌈ But to he or she whose desires are fulfilled
   And who knows the True Self
   Of Consciousness, Awareness, Love,
   All desires vanish like early morning mist
   Before the rising Sun,
   ⌊ Even here on Earth.

3. The understanding of what is Self,
   Is not gained by the Vedas,
   Nor by scholarship
   Or scriptural learning.
   He whom the Self
   Of Atman-Brahman chooses,
   Through Grace, by the apperception
   Of the Self as Consciousness,
   Then the Self chooses that body
   And makes it its own.

Self-Realization happens through grace – preliminary effort is
an aid and also comes about by grace.

4. Nor is that Self to be comprehended
   By one failing in strength,
   Earnestness, without power of attention.
   But if a wise man or woman

Strives earnestly,
With intelligence,
Then his understanding
As Self, enters the knowledge
Of Brahman as Consciousness.

5. When they have cognized
The Self fully,
Sages are satisfied.
They are conscious of
Consciousness.
Passions have retreated,
They are peaceful.
The wise having seen 'That'
Omnipresent everywhere,
Devoted to the Self
As Consciousness, Reality, Love,
Penetrate 'That' wholly.

6. Having well understood
The object of the knowledge
Of Advaita Vedanta,
Having purified their perception
By the Yoga of Surrender,
Enjoying Immortality,
All sages
Are free even at the time of dissolution
In the worlds of Brahman.

7.   Their manifold parts
     Re-enter their essential elements,
     Their senses into corresponding archetypes,
     Their acts and Self
     With their knowledge
     All become One in the
     Supreme Undying.

8.   As the flowing rivers vanish in the sea,
     Losing their very names and forms,
     So a sage freed from name and form
     Returns to the Supreme Brahman,
     Consciousness, Reality, Love,
     Greater than the greatest.

9.   He or she who knows 'That'
     Becomes 'That'.
     In his or her family no one is born
     Ignorant of this recognition,
     He or she conquers grief and wickedness.
     Free from the knot of the Heart
     He or she is Immortal.

10. This is declared by the verse
Of the Rig Veda:
'Let a man teach this
Science of Brahman to
Those who have performed
Preliminary spiritual practices
Of attention and concentration,
Who are well versed in the Vedas
Firmly established in the Heart
Who themselves offer
An offering to the great Rishi Agni,
Intermediary between the
Numinous world and the phenomenal,
Full of great faith,
And by whom the Fire Sacrifice
Has been witnessed,
According to the ancient
Vedic ceremony.'

11. Rishi Angiras taught
This True Science,
A man who is unprepared
Does not see it or understand it,
Adoration to the Ancient Rishis
Who revealed this perfect knowledge
Is adoration indeed!"

THE MANDUKYA UPANISHAD

Introduction

This short Upanishad belongs to the Atharva Veda. It is an exposition on the meaning of AUM. In the history of Advaita Vedanta it plays a most important part. Gaudapada, Shankara's teacher, wrote his famous commentary on this Upanishad (*The Karika*). This is the very first systematic exposition of Advaita. Shankara later commented on the Mandukya and *The Karika*.[47] Sir Edwin Arnold versified this splendid work into an English poem in his "In an Indian Temple".

Invocation

AUM,
Brilliant One, may we
Attend with our hearing
And listen to this most auspicious Upanishad,
May we see with our own
Apperception what is True.
May we be blest
By health, offer praise and complete
Our full gift of life in service
Of this Highest Teaching.

May Indra, King of the Gods
And all his pantheon assist us,
And grant us peace.

1. AUM
   This undying sacred word
   Encapsulates the whole of this universe,
   What has been
   What is now being
   What shall be
   All this is AUM
   And what is beyond these
   Three states of apparent time
   Past, present, future,
   That too is AUM.

2. All "That" truly is Brahman,
   The Self of Consciousness,
   Awareness, Love is Brahman,
   This Self has four divisions.[48]

3. The first is Vaisvanara,
   The waking state,
   Here, Consciousness is
   Turned outward,
   It has seven limbs,
   The head is light,

The eye is archetypal form,
The breath is the air of spaciousness,
The body is the whole.
The bladder is the prodigal wealth of Providence.
The feet are the ground of Earth,
The chest is the sacred place of sacrifice,
The hair is the sacred kusa grass,
The Heart,
The mind,
The mouth,
Are different aspects of fire.
Nineteen mouthed
Are the organs of the senses:
Hearing,
Touching,
Seeing,
Tasting,
Smelling.
The organs of action:
Speech,
Holding,
Movement,
Procreation,
Excretion.
The five vital breaths:
Reason,
Intellect,

Ego,
Thought patterns,
Self-Awareness.
It loves gross manifested
Apparent objects,
And thoroughly enjoys their sensation.

4. The second is Taijasa,
The dream state.
Here Consciousness
Is inward turned,
It shares the seven
Limbs and nineteen mouths of cognition.
It loves subtle, symbolic,
Subconscious objects,
And thoroughly enjoys
Their sensation.

5. The third is
Prajna, the deep sleep state,
Where one neither needs,
Wants, desires
Nor wishes for anything.
This state is without dreams.
Here one is undivided,
Unified
In an undifferentiated bliss

Of Consciousness,
Feeding on this peace,
His mouth is Consciousness.

6. "That" is the Lord of All,
    "That" the All-Knowing,
    "That" the Indwelling Ruler,
    "That" the Source,
    "That" is what is, the beginning and end
    Of all beings.

7. The fourth is the
    Turiya,
    The transcendental,
    Neither inward nor outward
    Turned Consciousness,
    Nor the two together,
    Nor an undifferentiated mass
    Of mind-spirit,
    Neither knowing
    Nor unknowing,
    Invisible,
    Ineffable,
    Intangible,
    Indescribable,
    Inconceivable,
    Indefinable,

It's sole essence being
Consciousness of its own
Self as Pure Consciousness.
Witnessing whatever happens,
It is the coming to peace
Of all relative, apparent existence,
Utterly still
Blissful love,
One without a second,
The Atman,
The Self,
The Pure Consciousness to be recognized.

8. This identical Atman or Self
   In the kingdom of sound is AUM.
   The four divisions of the
   Self are identical with its syllables.
   This is the explanation.

9. "A" is the waking state,
   It is the first and
   Encompasses all that is seen
   Outwardly,
   He who knows this embraces
   The desirable objects,
   He becomes the first.

10. "U" is the dream state.
It is an excellence
And contains the qualities of "A" and "M".
He who comprehends this
Glorifies the flow of philosophy
And rests in equilibrium.
In his family no one shall
Be ignorant of Consciousness
As Brahman, by reason of descent.

11. Prajna, deep sleep, is
The "M".
This is the capacity
Into which all enters.
He who understands this
Contains all and is contained
By all.

12. The fourth
Has no sound,
It is silence,
Unutterable,
Still
Yet dynamic,
A resting place from relative,
Apparent manifestation,
Blissful,

Compassionate,
All-loving,
Peaceful,
Without a trace of duality.
This AUM is the Atman-Brahman,
Pure Consciousness,
Self-Awareness.
He who apperceives "That"
Merges his ego in the Self,
Yes, he or she who understands
"That",
Peace – peace – peace.

Sri Bhagavan Ramana Maharshi lived largely in the fourth state or *turiya* and so was able to teach by silence, as did the primeval sage Dakshinamurti. Consciousness before realization is reflected because there is still identification by the egotistic will with the programmed thought patterns of the mind-body-feeling complex. After realization the pure Consciousness shines unimpeded as the pure witnessing Consciousness without identification. There is no "personal narcissistic ego" there any more, except as an object to be noticed. The functional part of the ego, the practical mind, goes on, but is witnessed.

THE PRAJNA UPANISHAD

Introduction

This Upanishad comes from the Atharva Veda. There are six fundamental questions put to the sage Pippalada by his disciples. Prajna means "question", so it is an Upanishad of Self-Enquiry.

Part 1

1. Sukesa, son of Bharadvaja
   Satya-Kama, son of Sibi,
   Gargya, grandson of Surya,
   Kausalya, son of Asvala,
   Bhargava from Vidarbha
   And Kabandhi, son of Katya
   Were all devoted disciples
   Seeking Brahman,
   Devoted,
   Firm,
   Earnest to find the Highest Truth.
   They believed the elderly sage Pippalada
   Could enlighten them.
   They therefore took gifts
   As pupils and approached
   Him with greatest respect.

2. The Rishi first told them:
    "Stay here and learn a year
    With austerity, restraint and faith,
    Then ask me any questions
    You may wish,
    If I know them
    I shall expound to you
    All I understand."

This verse emphasizes the need for a preparatory period to
train in spiritual practice and develop concentration, or the
power of inner attention, before embarking on the ultimate
teaching, that of Advaita Vedanta.

3. First, after a year of silence,
    Kabandhi approached and asked:
    "From where are all these
    Manifold creatures born?"

4. To Kabandhi, the Master
    Graciously answered:
    "Prajapati, the Source
    Of all Creation, Consciousness,
    Wished to manifest as potential energy
    So he could know his Self.
    He brooded,
    With his power,

He bifurcated
Into matter
And form
So as to create the Universe.

5. The Sun is a symbol
    Of the Life Force, or will,
    The Moon is a symbol of matter,
    Formed or formless,
    'What is' is formed
    By a combination of the elements,
    Through the creative power
    Of Consciousness.

6. Now to earthlings
    The Sun rises in the East,
    Apparently.
    He bathes all with his
    Life-giving rays.
    He then illumines North,
    South and West
    And bathes all creatures,
    Sentient and insentient,
    With his life-bestowing beams of glory.

7.   This fiery essence
     Assuming every form
     Renews itself from
     Moment to moment.

8.   'That' contains all
     Forms,
     The golden one,
     Omniscient,
     The goal,
     The light,
     The bestower of warmth,
     Possessing innumerable beams,
     Existing in countless forms,
     So rises the Sun,
     Symbol of the Life Force of all Creation.

9.   The Aeon is from the
     Source of Creation.
     There are two courses,
     Southern and Northern.
     The Northern route
     Is the lower teaching
     Of the Apara Vidya,
     The exoteric route
     Of tradition, religion.
     'Sacrificial and pious acts
     Are the orthodox work',

Speak the practitioners
Of the Northern route.
They win only the human world,
They transmigrate back to this plane,
Their tendencies inhabiting another body.
These Pundits, desirous of followers as their fruit,
Take this Northern route.
This is an Antique Path,
The way of materialism.

10.   But Sages who take
      The Southern route
      Of Para Vidya, the esoteric route,
      Enquire into the nature
      Of the Self as Consciousness,
      By austerity,
      Restraint,
      Faith
      And Knowledge,
      They gain the golden orb,
      The Sun of Truth
      That is truly the support
      Of all Life Breath and Force.
      'That' is Eternal, fearless,
      The Ultimate Understanding,
      From this there is no transmigration,
      Except into an auspicious being.

11.   The measurers of time
Call 'That' five footed.
The five seasons are his feet
As the Sun revolves,
The Father generates all.
He has twelve limbs
Corresponding to the lunar months.
He is the pull of water and their tides,
The substance above the heavens,
Above the sky.
Other calculators of apparent time
Say that the whole universe
Is fixed like spokes on the nave of a wheel,
Who as the embodiment of illusory Time
Is possessed of seven wheels
In the form of seven horses,
Endowed with six spokes of six seasons.
Whether possessor of five feet,
Twelve limbs, seven wheels or
Six spokes,
It is the Aeon,
The embodiment of the mystery
Of Time,
Ruler of Creatures
Led by the Sun
And the Moon,
Which causes a world of illusion.

This verse is a poetical mystic revelation or vision and escapes most commentators except Shankara, who explains the process of apparent time in some detail.

12. The lunar month
    Is also a Ruler of Creation.
    The dark half is material,
    The bright half is life.
    This is why Rishis
    Perform their sacrifices in the light,
    Fools in the dark.

13. Day and Night
    Are also Rulers of Creation.
    Day is life,
    Night is material.
    They who enjoy
    Intercourse by day
    Waste their vital energy,
    Those that enjoy sex at night
    Are wise indeed for they are controlled.

14. Food is also a Ruler of Creation.
    From their essence flows semen,
    From this seed new creatures are born.

15. Those who practise sensual enjoyment,
    Bear sons and daughters,
    To them alone is the delight
    Of the created world,
    Where restraint, control
    And truth are stabilized.

16. To them is that pure world
    In which there is no criminality,
    Falsehood, lying or deceit."

Part 2

1. Then Bhargava from Vidarbha
   Asked Pippalada,
   With great respect:
   "How many powers maintain
   The worlds of Creation?
   How many illuminate them?
   Who among the powers is Supreme?"

2. The Master replied:
   "Ether truly has such power,
   Wind,
   Fire,
   Water,
   Earth,

Speech,
Mind,
Eye,
Ear,
It has illumined them all.
They proclaim:
'Together we sustain and maintain this body.'

3. The Force of Life
   Said:
   'Do not harbour such
   Delusion.
   I, alone,
   Splitting myself fivefold
   Into the senses,
   Sustain and maintain
   This body.'

4. They did not believe him.
   Through pride he mounted
   Upward in the body,
   When he went up all
   The others also rose,
   When he calmed down
   So did the others.
   So as all bees rise
   When the Queen flies

And as they calm down
When she settles,
So the senses being
Satisfied praise the Force of Life.

The force of life, *élan vital* or will, feels as if it is rising up the
body when it asserts itself; this can be experienced by all, a
great deal of the time.

5. As fire he burns,
    He blazes as the Sun,
    Bestows the great gift of rain,
    Blows the winds,
    Animates the Earth,
    Matter and Gods.
    He is being and non-being,
    Immortal.

6. As spokes in the centre
    Of the wheel,
    Everything and everyone is fixed
    By their Life Force,
    The Rig Veda,
    The Blessings,
    The Chants,
    The Sacrifices,
    Courage and Wisdom.

7. As the Lord of Creatures,
   The Force of Life
   Moves in the Womb
   Then there is a new birth
   With tendencies included.
   Oh Life Force,
   All creatures on Earth
   Bring offerings to you who
   Dwells amongst the vital breaths.

8. You are the head bearer
   Of offerings to the body,
   You are the first offering
   To the ancestors,
   You are the true
   Spiritual Practice of the Seers,
   The descendants of Atharva
   And Angiras.

This is a great hymn to the life force, unparalleled in world poetry.

9. You are
   King Indra,
   Oh Life Force,
   By thy strength
   You are Rudra

As guardian,
You move in the atmosphere
Of space as a Sun,
The Lord of Lights.

10. When you shed rain
The creatures sigh blissfully
Knowing there will be
The substance they desire.

11. You are ever pure,
Oh Life Force,
The One Seed,
The Devourer,
The True Lord of All.
We give of our food to be eaten,
All pervading Space,
You are our Father.

12. Your form is established
In speech,
In hearing,
In seeing,
Which dwells always in the mind-brain.
Bless us with auspiciousness,
Never desert us.

13. All this manifestation
Is governed by this Will,
The Life Force.
Guard us as a gracious Mother
Guards her dear sons,
Grant us your beneficial Providence
And Wisdom."

These verses give us an insight into the cast of mind of an ancient civilization. No less a philosopher than Friedrich Nietzsche believed that the Vedic civilization was far superior to the Christian because it was based on the aristocratic values of the rishis with an ordered society protected by warriors. He thought the Laws of Manu superior to the Laws of Moses. This life force is close to his "Will to Power" and the Schopenhauerian Will, the solution to the riddle of the universe, as he wrote in his *World as Will and Idea*, a book highly influenced by the Upanishads, according to his own admission. So this hymn is not only rhapsodic, it also points to philosophic truth. If the will is egotistic it is either negated by ascetic practice, Self-Enquiry, or destroyed by surrendering to the divine will through grace, not by the individual's arrogant idea can he destroy the will by his own effort.

Part 3

1. Then Kausalya respectfully
   Asked Pippalada:
   "How is this Life Force generated?
   How does it enter the body?
   How is it distributed there?
   And maintained?
   How does it leave?
   How does it support the outside?
   How does it support
   What relates to the Self?"

2. Pippalada replied:
   "You are asking very high
   Questions indeed,
   But as you are devoted
   To knowing the Truth of Brahman
   I will inform you.

3. This Life Force is born from the
   Self, Consciousness, Reality, Love.
   The person is a mere shadow,
   The Self is the Sun.
   It enters the body through mental activity.

4. As a general instructs his
   Officers, commanding them:
   'Govern this and that town',
   So does the Life Force allocate
   Vital breath to the respective organs.

5. The exhalation is in the organs
   Of excretion and generation,
   The Life Breath is in the eye,
   Ear, mouth, and nose.
   In the centre is the equalizing breath,
   It affects eating and digesting of food.
   From this arises seven flames.

6. In the Heart is the Self.
   There are a hundred and one arteries,
   To each belong another hundred,
   From which belong
   Seventy-two thousand arteries,
   Within moves the equalized distributed breath.

Like Ancient China, with its acupunctural science, the Vedic civilization had an experimental knowledge of the vast complexities inherent in the human body. *Nadis* were nerve centres, which were part of the ancient Ayurvedic medical system which is still practised very effectively in East and West.

7. Now, mounting upwards,
   Through an inhalation,
   This leads to good wishes
   To the perfect world of manifestation
   In equilibrium,
   Where all is good,[49]
   Wickedness trashes
   On the world,
   The consequences of both good and evil
   Affect the world of men and women.

8. The glorious, magnificent,
   Blazing orange Sun
   Arises to illuminate outside life
   And assists, kindly, the Life Breath,
   In your eye.
   The God inherent in the Earth's core
   Supports your exhalation, every moment,
   What lives between Sun and Earth
   Is this equalizing breath.
   The air we breath is the same breath, diffused.

9. Fire is the inhalation,
   He whose fire of Life Force ends transmigrates
   When senses are held by the mind.

10. With one's thoughts turning
    One enters into life.
    His Life Force and fire
    Along with Self, Consciousness, Brahman,
    Leads to whatever world
    Created by 'That' thought.

11. The Sage who knows
    Life to be the acceptance
    Of 'what is'
    Will never lack disciples.
    He becomes Immortal.

The world is an illusion created by the organ of cognition
(mind-brain). This doctrine of maya is found in Buddhism,
Hinduism, and Western Idealist Philosophy (Berkeley, Kant,
Schopenhauer, Bradley, etc.).

12. The birth,
    The doorway,
    The house,
    The fivefold Lordship,[50]
    The relationships of life to Self,
    Knowing all this
    One becomes Immortal."

Part 4

1. Then Gargya asked Pippalada:
   "What is it that sleeps in the individual?
   What keeps awake in him or her?
   What God enjoys the dreams?
   Whose is the enjoyment?
   To whom is all this happening?"

2. Pippalada replied:
   "As all sunbeams
   At sunset become one
   And then spread out at dawn,
   So does this all become One
   In the Supreme.
   In that state
   The person does not hear,
   See,
   Smell,
   Taste,
   Touch,
   Speak,
   Taste,
   Rejoice,
   Emit,
   Or move.
   He sleeps.

3. The fires of Life Force alone
   Burn in this City.
   The householder's fire is the exhalation,
   The southern sacrificial
   Fire is the retention,
   Inhalation is the fire of
   The offering.

4. Retained breath
   Equalizes the inhalation
   And exhalation.
   The fruit of the sacrifice
   Is the inhalation.
   The ego is the sacrifice,
   It leads to Brahman every day.

Life is seen as a sacrifice – in modern terms the ego is
sacrificed or surrendered to God or the Self or Consciousness.
The ancient science of pranayama is invoked here. Verse 5
refers to dreams.

5. In sleep, God ruling as mind
   Experiences majesty.
   He or she sees again the objects,
   He or she recalls
   Whatever he or she has heard,
   Whatever he or she has experienced,
   He enjoys all and is all he sees.

6. When overwhelmed
    By light of the Self,
    Then the ruler God of mind
    Does not dream,
    Happiness arises.

As in dreamless sleep – an analogy of Self-Realization, or the
no-mind state. See also the Mandukya Upanishad.

7. Even as beautiful birds
    Fly to a tree and rest,
    So do all here fly
    To the Supreme Self,
    Where they find rest
    In dreamless sleep.

8. There is Earth,
    Water,
    Fire,
    Air,
    Ether,
    Seeing,
    Hearing,
    Smelling,
    Tasting,
    Touching
    The phallus,

And what can be enjoyed,
The organ of excretion
And what can be expected,
The feet and its walking,
The mind-brain and what can
Be cognized.
The sense of Self-Awareness
And its connection,
Thinking and what can be thought,
Radiance and what can be lit up,
Life Breath and all it supports.

This is a statement of the Sankhya philosophic categories, five
cosmic elements and ten organs of action.

9. He truly is a Seer,
   A Rishi who sees,
   Hears,
   Smells,
   Farts,
   Perceives,
   Conceives,
   Acts,
   Whose essence
   Is Self-Knowledge,
   The Supreme Person
   Who dwells in

The imperishable Self
Of Consciousness, Reality, Love.

10. He who knows
The shadowless,
Bodiless,
Transparent,
Pure,
Imperishable
Self,
Touches the Supreme Atman-Brahman,
Self of Consciousness,
Reality, Love.
He who knows 'That' Self
In which resides intelligence,
Vital breaths,
The elements,
The divine powers,
Omniscience,
Enters the 'All'."

Part 5

1. Then Satya-Kama asked
Pippalada: "What world does he or she
Achieve by meditating
On the meaning of AUM?"

2. Pippalada replied:
    "AUM is both the unlimited
    Absolute Brahman
    And the limited Isvara,
    The Personal God.

The higher (*para vidya*) and lower (*apara vidya*) are reconciled
in this verse as a concession. In the absolute teaching, God is
impersonal, and in the exoteric teaching there is a personal
God. But both admit the Sat-Guru, the true "guru" immanent
in the heart, who silently guides the devotee to Self-
Realization in due course.

3. If he meditates even on the 'A',
    He may be enlightened by grace of 'That'
    But his tendencies
    May transmigrate to Earth
    After leaving the body.
    The Rig Veda leads him
    To the world of mankind.
    Blessed with restraint,
    Celibacy and faith,
    He experiences magnificence.

4. If he meditates on 'AU'
    He reaches the subtle intellect,
    He is led by the Vedic rules
    To that middle space

Of the Inner World,
He knows magnificence
There and returns to Earth.

5. But if he meditates on
   AUM
   He unites with solar light,
   Even as the snake casts off his skin
   He throws off his ropes of bondage.
   He is led by sacred chants
   To the world of Brahman,
   He sees 'That' which dwells
   In the body,
   Higher than the highest.

6. AUM when arriving at death,
   If the sound is chanted,
   Is used for initiating actions,
   Well carried out,
   Outside,
   Inside,
   Or in-between,
   This knower never doubts.

7. With the Rig Veda
   One reaches this world of Brahman.
   With the Vedic rules
   He reaches the inner space.

With the sacred chants
He reaches 'That'
Which Rishis recognize,
'That' the Sage realizes
With AUM sounding
As support,
Which is calm,
Undying,
Immortal,
Fearless,
Supreme."

AUM is the primeval sound whereby creation emanated from the original impulse of potential energy wishing to manifest the Source. The Mandukya Upanishad and *Karika of Gaudapada* (a commentary) discuss the meaning of AUM in depth. Both are published by the Ramakrishna Vedanta Centre.

Part 6

1. Sukesa then said
   To Pippalada:
   "Itwanya-Nabha, a Prince
   Of Kosela, asked if I knew
   The Supreme Person[51] with sixteen parts?
   I told him I did not. I would
   Never lie to you for that would
   Be my spiritual death."

2. Pippalada answered:
"Here within 'this' body
The Supreme Person of the sixteen
Parts arises.

3. That Supreme Person pondered
In himself
In whose departure
Shall I be departing?
In whose settling down
Shall I be settling down?

This chapter describes the *linga-sariva* or the subtle body of the Sankhya system of philosophy. Verse 3 opens up the process of Self-Enquiry. It is the subtle body that transmigrates at death back to Consciousness. The ego or sense of separate individuality is centred in the brain and decomposes with the body.

4. 'That' created Life
From the Life Breath,
Faith,
Ether,
Air,
Light,
Water,
Earth,

Senses,
Mind,
Food,
From food essences,
Vital energy,
Restraint,
Hymns,
Deeds,
Worlds
And their names.

5. As swift running rivers
   Flood into the ocean,
   Then merge losing name and form,
   So Sages with their sixteen principles
   Merge with Brahman,
   On reaching 'That',
   Are dissolved.
   'That One' is without divisions,
   Immortal.

6. In whom the parts
   Are all well fixed as spokes
   In the nave of a wheel,
   Know him as 'That'
   To be known,
   Then death will not affect you."

7. To the devotees Pippalada said:
   "Only this far do I
   Comprehend the Supreme Brahman.
   There is nothing higher
   Than 'That'."

8. The devotees then sang
   His praises:
   "You are indeed a Great Guru
   Who has taken us from ignorance
   To the other shore, free from illusion.
   Hail all Sages of the
   Supreme,
   All hail!"

Prof. S. Radhakrishnan likens this to a verse by Christina
Rossetti:

Lord, we are rivers running to Thy sea,
Our waves and ripples all derived from Thee,
A nothing we should have, a nothing be
Except of Thee.

FROM THE BRIHADARANYAKA UPANISHAD

An important Upanishad, which belongs to the *Satapatha Brahmana*, the Brihadaranyaka is one of the longest of all in this sacred library. I have therefore made a careful abridgement, in line with many translations, from only the first two books. Shankara made an extensive commentary.

BOOK I

Part 1

This Vedic section, identifying the universe with the sacrificial horse, has been omitted, as it is in most modern translations.

Part 2

This is a poetic "Hymn of Creation", anthropomorphic in character.

1. In the beginning
    There was nothing
    To be perceived.
    Through Death
    All was hidden
    By hunger.
    Death is hunger,
    Death, the primordial being,
    Contemplated
    And wished for a body,
    Then he moved in pensive worship,
    From brooding and pondering came water.
    He reflected again,
    Truly, from my worship came water,
    Now there is living water
    For he or she who understands
    "That".

2. What was there as froth
    On the surface of the water
    Hardened and became Earth.
    On that crust Death rested
    And from resting in heat
    Fire, Agni, full of flame raged.

3. Fire divided into a triad.
    As Aditya, the Sun,
    Vayu, the air,
    Spirit, Prajna.
    The head was the East,
    The arms North-East and South-East,
    The tail the West, the two legs
    The North-West and South-West.
    The sides were South and North.
    The back, the heavens,
    The belly, the sky,
    The dust, the Earth.
    Thus he, Death, Mrityu,
    Stands firm in living water
    And he or she who knows "That"
    Also stands firm.

4. Death wished for a second body,
    He embraced the notion of speech.
    The time of pregnancy was one year,
    So speech, the Master, carried
    Him for twelve months,
    Then Time gave him birth.
    Death opened his mouth
    As if to swallow him,
    He shouted, "Bhan!"
    And became speech.

The hymn moves into a mythological dimension reminding one of the Ancient Greek myths.

5. Death pondered,
   If I kill him I will have no food.
   He therefore mothered this speech
   And fathered it by the
   Verses of all the Vedas,
   The poetic meters,
   Sacrifices,
   Mankind,
   The animal kingdoms.

6. He wished to sacrifice
   Once more
   With a worthier sacrifice.
   He laboured and performed austerities,
   A glorious power left him,
   The Prajna, Life Force,
   Through the senses.
   Then when the senses had left,
   The body became pregnant again with swelling,
   Now the mental powers were in the body.

7. He wished his body
   To be fit for sacrifice
   And that he should be in it.
   So he became a horse

Because it swelled
And was fit for sacrifice.
Then freeing the horse
He pondered.
After one year he
Sacrificed the horse
For himself
Along with other animals
To the Gods.
That is why priests
Sacrifice to Prajapati,
A sanctified horse,
Dedicated to all the Gods.
He who shines there is
The horse sacrifice.
His body is the year,
This fire is Arka,[52]
Its limbs are the world.
So fire and Sun are Arka
And the horse sacrifice.
They also become the same
God of Death.
He who knows "That"
Conquers Death
And touches Immortality.

Part 3

Verses 26 are omitted by many translators for brevity as they mainly concern bodily functions, the superiority of life breath, and the worth of the Sama Veda (musical hymns).

27. He who knows "That"
    Is the support of the Saman
    And is supported.
    Its support is speech,
    The breath is sung as Saman,
    Next follows the Abhyaroba,
    The ascension of the Paramana verses.
    The Priest begins to chant the Saman
    And when he starts the sacrifice
    Recites the sacred Yagus verses.

Now follows one of the most sacred mantras in the Upanishads.

> Lead me from the unreal
> To the Real!
> Lead me from darkness
> To Light!
> Lead me from Death
> To Immortality!
> The unreal is Death,
> The real is Immortality,

As in darkness, ignorance and death,
Light is Self-Knowledge,
Immortality.

28. Next come other verses
    For obtaining food.
    The sacrifices may also
    Request a boon.
    The priest recognizes
    The efficacy of the sacrifice.
    This knowledge conquers all worlds,
    Fear of Death vanishes forever.

Part 4

1. In the beginning
   The Universe was the Self,
   Pure Consciousness, alone;
   There was the image
   Of an archetypal man,
   Purusha.
   Looking around he saw nothing
   Other than his own Self.
   He uttered, "This is I-I,"
   So he became I-I by name.
   Then if a man or woman
   Is asked "Who are you?"

He or she replies, "This is I,"
And then his other name,
Before the Self destroyed
By fire all evils.
Therefore he was named "man",
Purusha.
He who knows this burns down
Anyone who tries to supplant him.

The verse echoes the biblical phrase that "man was created in the image of God", a microcosm in the macrocosm. This idea is also found in the Kabbalah. The Self-Enquiry of Ramana Maharshi asks the question "Who Am I?" and ends with the recognition "I am That". I-I is the Self; I refers to the fictitious personal identity.

2. He was afraid,
   In his aloneness,
   But then reflected,
   "As there is nothing but my Self
   Of pure Consciousness
   Why should I fear?"
   His fear vanished.
   Truly fear arises from
   The idea of a second.

Fear is inherent once duality is believed in. Non-duality is fearless.

3. He felt no delight being alone.
   He wished for a mate,
   With a wife there was enlargement.
   He then divided the Self.
   So arose as archetypes
   Husband and wife.
   Yagnavalkya said,
   "We two are like halves of a shell,"
   Now the void which was there
   Is filled by a wife.
   He embraced her
   And mankind was generated.

4. She reflected,
   "How can he continue
   To embrace me
   As I came from his own Self?
   I shall hide."
   She transformed herself
   Into an archetypal heifer.
   He became an archetypal bull.
   So they came together
   And cattle were generated.
   Then she became an archetypal mare,
   He an archetypal stallion.
   He embraced her
   And one-hoofed horses, mules

And deer were born.
Then she became an archetypal ewe,
He became an archetypal ram.
He embraced her,
Goats and sheep were generated.
They went on procreating
In archetypal pairs down to the insect kingdom,
Hence ants were born.

5. He said,
    "I am this Creation
    For I was its Creator,"
    He became the Creation.
    Whoever knows this
    Lives well in his Creation.

6. Then he made fire by friction.
    He blew with his mouth
    And rubbed sticks together by hand.
    This is why the mouth and palms are hairless.
    And when people say,
    "Sacrifice to this God, or that God"
    Each God is his manifestation,
    He is all Gods.
    Whatever is moist
    He made from seed,
    This is Soma.[53]

In this Universe there is
Either food
Or consumer of food.
Soma is the drink,
Agni is the drinker.
This is the high Creation of Brahman
When he created the Gods
From his own Self
When he was mortal, as Sacrificer,
He created the Immortals.
It is thus the highest Creation.
He who knows this lives
In his own highest Creation,
His own Self, as Consciousness.

7. Now all was unevolved,
    It became evolved through having form
    And by being named.
    He called "So and So"
    Is such a One.
    Brahman or the Self as
    Consciousness
    Entered to the very tips
    Of the fingernails.
    As a razor
    Fitted its case,
    Or as fire settles in the hearth,

He is invisible,
But when breathing,
He is breath by name,
Similarly with speaking and speech,
Seeing and eye,
Hearing and ear,
Thinking and brain.
All these are the names of his deeds.
He who worships him as one or the other
Fails to understand or know him.
Let men indeed worship him as Self,
As Self, as Consciousness,
For in "That" All is One.
Consciousness is the substratum
Of all things.
Through "That" one understands all.
And as all, one can find "That" again,
By its footsteps,
Like one traces cattle that were lost.
So he who knows "That"
Finds glory, vision and praise.

8. "That" which is nearer
To us than anything else,
Dearer than a son or wealth,
Anyone who declares any other
Than his Self as Consciousness as dearer

Will lose what is dear to him first.
He who worships the Self as dear
The object of his love will never die.

9. The Sages say:
"Men think,
Through the knowledge of Brahman
We shall become Infinite Existence."
Let them ask themselves,
"What did 'That' Brahman
As Consciousness know by
Which 'That' became Infinite
Existence, the All?"[54]

10. Truly in the initial act of Creation
This was Brahman,
"That" Brahman knew its Self
Saying, "I am Brahman, Reality
Consciousness, Love."
From "That" all sprang.
So whatever God was awakened
To know Brahman
Became "That" Brahman,
As with the Rishis, men and women.
Rishi Vamadeva realized "That" singing,
"I was as the Moon,
I was as the Sun."

So he who knows that he or she
Is Brahman as Consciousness,
His or her true nature,
Becomes all Infinite Existence,
And even the Gods cannot stop
"That" happening
For Brahman is their Self.
Now if a man or woman worships another God,
Believing the God is One,
And he or she another,
A separate entity,
He or she is no better than a beast to the Gods.
Just as many beasts nourish a man,
So do men nourish the Gods.
If only one beast is taken away
It is regretted,
And more when many are taken.
It is the same with men and women
To the Gods.
Maybe they do not wish
Men and women to know this.

Creation "sprang" as when a stone is dropped into a pool from a height; all the ripples follow inevitably and consequentially from that act, until the pool is calm again, and another stone is dropped and a new universe appears, ad infinitum. Men and women are no better than cattle (beasts) to the gods unless they remember who they really are, the Self of Consciousness, and live from that standpoint, not from separation. This understanding is "awakening" from sleep.

11.   Truly in the very beginning
      "That" was Brahman,
      One, alone.
      That One was not willing
      To govern the Universe
      On his own.
      He created excellent
      Archetypal forces as Gods.
      Indra, Varuna, Soma, Rudra,
      Parganya, Yama, Mrityu and
      Isvara.
      There is nothing beyond these
      Natural forces ...

The rest of verses 11–13 are omitted as they are about places in ritual ceremonies and orders of deities in the Vedic pantheon.

14.   He created still further
      The Law of Righteousness, Dharma.
      Law is upheld by the power of the
      Warrior,
      There is nothing superior

To this Law.
Even a weak man can rule a stronger
With the aid of the Law,
As with the aid of a king.
Thus the Dharmic Law is True.

15. If a man or woman leaves the body
Without having seen his true future life
As Consciousness, the Self,
Then that Consciousness being unknown
Does not bless him.
It is as if the Vedas had not been read
Or a good deed had been omitted.
Even if one who does not know his own Self
Performs some great holy work,
It will die for him in the end.
Let a man worship the Self
As Consciousness, Brahman, Peace,
Love, as his own true nature.
Then his work will endure
For whatever he desires
Comes from the Self.

The first part of this verse again gives minute details of the Vedic pantheon. This section I have omitted in order to concentrate on the teaching.

16. Truly this egotistic self
    Of the ignorant man or woman
    Is to be enjoyed
    By all created beings.
    If he sacrifices and worships
    He is of the celestial world.
    If he chants hymns
    He is of the world of the Ancient Sages.
    If he makes offerings to the Ancestors
    And wishes for family he is of their world.
    If he gives shelter and food to guests
    He is of the world of mankind.
    If he feeds animals, he is of their world.
    If ants, birds, and pets live in his house
    He is of their world.
    As everyone trusts
    His world will not be hurt,
    He who knows this will escape injury.
    This is truly known and examined by reason.

17. In the beginning
    All was Self, alone One.
    A wife wishes to bring forth offspring and wealth
    To perform rites and sacrifices.
    Until this happens she is incomplete.
    Consciousness is Self,
    Speech is the wife,

[221]

The Life Force the child,
The eye is wealth.
Hearing through the ear
The body performs the rite,
So there are five factors,
As with mankind, the animals,
And all that exists.
He who knows "That"
Obtains all "That".

Part 5

Verses 1–16 are largely anthropomorphic and are omitted, as in most abridgements.

17. When a man thinks he will die
    He says to his son,
    "Thou art Brahman,
    Thou art the sacrifice,
    Thou art the world."
    The son replies,
    "I am Brahman,
    I am the sacrifice,
    I am the world."
    Whatever has been learned
    By the father, "That"
    Taken as One is Brahman,

As with the rites and the world.
A son who is taught to do all this
Is a world son, a lokya.
When the father dies
His own spirit enters into his son
And any deed done amiss by the father
Is exonerated by the son.
By help of his son
The father stands firm
And the immortal spirits
Of speech, mind and breath
Come to him.

18. From Earth
    And fire,
    Divine speech
    Comes to him,
    And whatever he says
    Comes to be.

19. From heaven and the Sun
    Divine mind enters,
    He becomes joyful
    And grieves no longer.

20. From water and the Moon
    Divine breath enters
    "That" is divine breath
    Which moving or still
    Never tires and never dies.
    He who knows "That" becomes
    The Self of all beings.
    As Hiranyagarbha is,
    So he becomes,
    And as all beings know to honour
    That God with rites,
    So do all beings honour who knows "That".
    Whatever sorrow the creatures
    Endure stays with them,
    Only good follows after he or she
    Who knows "That"
    Evil never touches the Gods.

Hiranyagarbha is Brahman reduced to the concept of a cosmic soul between Isvara (personal God who rules the world) and the soul of mankind. This reductionism is a lesser teaching, the *apara vidya*. For the pure Advaitin, all is Brahman, the *para vidya*. Many teachers who do understand these distinctions are best described as "neo-Advaitins", a Western adaptation (culturally conditioned) of the original Upanishadic teaching given by Shankara and Ramana Maharshi.

21.   The Father created more actions
       Possible through the senses.
       When they had been formed
       They strove amongst themselves.
       The voice proclaimed, "I will speak,"
       The eye said, "I shall see,"
       The ear held, "I shall hear,"
       And so all the senses spoke
       According to their nature.
       Death having become tired, seized them,
       And held them back from the world.
       So speech, eye and ear grew tired.
       But Death never took away the Life Breath
       So the others strived to know "That"
       And said, "He is the best of us;
       Whether moving or still,
       'That' never wearies or dies.
       Let us all take his form."
       So they are also called spirits.
       In whichever household
       A man or woman who knows "That"
       Is the named head of the family.
       He who opposes any who doubts "That"
       Will perish and die, as shall the mortal body.

22. The God Agni declared, "I shall burn,"
    Aditya the Sun beamed, "I shall warm,"
    Kandramas, the Moon chanted, "I shall shine,"
    And all the other Gods sang
    According to their nature.
    As it was with the Life Breath
    So it was with Vayu, wind, amongst
    These Gods.
    Other deities fade, not Vayu,
    Air never fades.

23. "That" from whom the Sun dawns
    And into which it sets
    Also rises from the breath
    And sets in it.

Part 6

1. Truly this is threefold,
   Name,
   Form,
   Work.
   Of these, name is speech,
   It is the Uktha Hymn of Origin,
   From it all names arise.
   It is their song, the same as all names.
   It is their Brahman prayer,
   It supports all names.

2. Of all forms
   The eye is the Uktha Hymn
   From which all forms arise.
   It is their song, the same as all forms.
   It is their Brahmanic prayer,
   It supports all forms of all works.
   The body is the Uktha Hymn
   From which all works arise,
   It is their song
   For it is the same as all works.
   It is their Brahmanic prayer,
   It supports all works.
   "That" being threefold
   Is in reality One,
   This Self, Consciousness,
   The Self being One is this triad.
   "That" is the Eternal,
   Clothed by the Truth,
   Truly breath is Immortal,
   Name and form are Truth,
   By them the Eternal is enrobed.

BOOK II

Part 1

1.   Once there was a wise man
     Named Gargya Balaki;
     A man of great learning.
     He said to Agatasatru of Kasi,
     "Shall I teach you Brahman?"
     Agatasatru answered,
     "We will offer a thousand
     Cows for that knowledge,
     For truly people come
     Saying a second King Janaka is here."

King Janaka was an enlightened monarch, Self-Realized by the sage Ashtavakra. The *Ashtavakra Gita* gives his teaching. This was a beloved text of Ramana Maharshi and Robert Adams. Ramesh Balsekar has written a masterful commentary on this scripture, *Duet for One*, Advaita Press.

2.   Gargya said,
     "'That' which is the Sun
     'That' I adore as Brahman."
     Agatasatru replied,
     "No, no, do not talk like this,
     I worship 'That' truly

As the Supreme
Chief of All Being,
King of the Universe.
Who adores him so becomes himself
Chief of All Beings,
King of the Universe."

3. "'That' which is in the
Moon and in the mind
I love as Brahman."
Agatasatru replied, "No, no!
Do not speak of him simply like this.
I truly love him as the Magnificent One
Clad in white robes as Soma, the God,
Whoever loves him so,
Soma, the divine wine of ecstasy,
Is poured out for him daily,
His spiritual food never fails."

4. Gargya said, "'That'
Which is in the lightning flash
And deep in the Heart
I love as Brahman."
Agatasatru contradicted again,
"No, no!
Never speak to me like this.
I love him truly as 'That'

Luminosity and radiance.
Whomsoever loves him so becomes
Shining and radiant,
His children also are golden."

5. Gargya said, "'That'
In the ether and Heart
I worship as Brahman."
Agatasatru replied,
"No, no!
Do not talk to me like this.
I worship 'That' which is
The plenitude, and still.
Whoever worships him as 'That'
Becomes fulfilled,
As do his family and herds,
His children never perish from this world."

6. Gargya said, "'That'
Which is in the wind
I adore as Brahman."
Agatasatru said, "No, no, again.
Do not talk to me like this.
I adore 'That' as unconquerable,
Indra, King of the Gods.
Whoever so loves him becomes
Victorious, invincible, conquering all his foes."

7. Gargya said, "'That'
    Which is in the fire
    And in the Heart
    I worship as Brahman."
    Agatasatru said, "No! No!
    Do not talk like this.
    I worship 'That' as all powerful,
    Whoever worships him as 'That'
    Becomes all powerful along
    With his offspring."

8. Gargya said, "'That'
    Which is the water, the seed,
    And Heart I love as Brahman."
    Agatasatru said, "No! No!
    Never speak like this.
    I love him as 'That' which reflects
    His own Nature
    Not by what does not reflect
    In this way.
    Whoever loves him in this way
    Will have children
    Who reflect their own true Nature too."

9.   Gargya said, "'That'
     Which is seen in the mirror
     I revere as Brahman."
     Agatasatru said, "No! No! Again.
     Do not talk in this way.
     I revere him as the Brilliant One.
     Whoever respects him so
     Becomes brilliant.
     His children shine brilliantly
     And with whomever he meets
     He outshines."

10. Gargya said, "The sound 'That'
     Pursues a person
     When he or she moves,
     'That' I praise as Brahman."
     Agatasatru again said,
     "No! No!
     Do not speak to me like this,
     I praise him truly as
     Consciousness, Reality, Love,
     Sat, Chit, Ananda,
     Whoever praises him thus
     Reaches his full age in this life,
     Breath does not leave prematurely."

11. Gargya said, "'That'
     Which is space
     I love as Brahman."
     Agatasatru contradicted him,
     "No, no!
     Never speak to me like this.
     I love 'That' truly as
     The second who never leaves us,
     The One.
     Who so loves him so becomes
     Possessed of 'That',
     He is never separated from the One."

12. Gargya said, "'That'
     Who consists
     Of the shadow,
     That I adore as Brahman."
     Agatasatru said, "No, no
     Do not talk this way.
     I adore him truly as Death.
     Whoever sees 'That' reaches
     His full life span in the world,
     Death does not come before his time."

13. Gargya spoke, "'That'
     Which is the Spirit,
     In the subtle intellect and the Heart,
     'That' I revere as Brahman."

[233]

Agatasatru disagreed again,
"No! No!
Do not talk like this.
I revere him truly as
One who has realized the Self
As Consciousness, Reality, Love,
Sat, Chit, Ananda.
Whoever realizes him so
Will also come to Self-Realization
As will his offspring."
And so Gargya held his
Peace and ceased.

14. Agatasatru questioned,
"This far only?"
"Thus far only," Gargya replied.
Agatasatru said, "This is
Not sufficient to know 'That',
The true Brahman."
Gargya answered, "Let me please come
To you as a pupil then."

15. Agatasatru said,
"Really it is unusual that
A Brahmin
Should come to a Warrior
For knowledge of Brahman.

However I will teach you clearly."
So speaking he held him by the hand,
As they walked they came
Across a man asleep.
Agatasatru addressed the
Sleeping man,
"Oh great one, dressed in a
White robe, Soma[55] King."
The man did not arise.
Then Agatasatru touched him with his hand
And the man woke up.

16. Agatasatru said,
   "When this man was asleep
   Where was then the Consciousness?
   And the intelligence?
   And from where did he return?"
   Gargya said, "I do not know."

17. Agatasatru said,
   "When this man was asleep,
   Where was then the Consciousness,
   Which through the mind and senses
   Absorbed within himself all intelligence
   'That' lies in the ethereal space
   Which is in the Heart,
   The Real Self, the Brahman?

When he absorbs these different
Masks of intelligence in his Self
It is said that he sleeps.
Then breath,
Speech,
Hearing,
Seeing,
Thinking,
Are retained inwardly.

18. But when the brain
Moves in sleep
He dreams.
These are his words.
He is a Great King,
A Great Brahmin,
He reigns, he falls,
And as a Great King rules his subjects,
Moves about to his pleasure,
Within his own kingdom.
So does the individual
Endowed with intelligence
Retain the senses
And move about pleasurably
Within his own body while dreaming.

19. Then when he is deep in sleep
    He knows nothing.
    There are seventy-two thousand
    Arteries called nadis, which emerge
    From the Heart
    And spread through the whole body.

20. Through them he moves
    And rests
    Just as a youth,
    Or a King or Brahmin
    Having reached the peak of happiness
    Might rest fully refreshed.

21. As the spider emerges with silk
    Or as sparks fly out from fire,
    So do all senses,
    Worlds, Gods, beings,
    Emerge from the Self,
    Consciousness, Awareness,
    Reality, Peace, Brahman, Love.
    This Upanishad is the Truth,
    The Teaching of 'That' Self
    Is the Truth of the Truth.
    Truly the senses are True,
    And he or she is the Truth of the True."

Part 2

Part 2 is omitted by many translators in the abridgement of this Upanishad. The metaphors are mainly drawn from the Atharva Veda Samhita X: 8–9 and concern the relationship of the subtle body and the head in analogous language drawn from the Vedas.

Part 3 discusses the advanced philosophic concept between the phenomenal world and the noumenal world, later taken up by Plato. It is known that the Ancient Greeks had links with India, as references in Josephus show: "The Indian gymnophysicists visited Athens, etc." The early Greek philosophers, such as the Pythagoreans, echo the Upanishads, as does the later neo-Platonist, Plotinus. This distinction between the numinous and phenomenal was later stressed by Immanuel Kant, the founder of modern Western philosophy.

Part 3

1. There are two aspects of Brahman,
    Firstly material, phenomenal,
    Visible,
    Secondly immaterial, numinous,
    Invisible,
    The mortal, death-bound, solid,
    The Immortal, deathless, liquid.
    Sat, being, Reality

And tya "That"
Sat-tya, the Truth,
Reality.

2. All except air,
    Pneumatic, transparent,
    And sky, the space,
    Consciousness,
    Are material,
    Are mortal,
    Are solid
    And can be defined.
    The essence of "That"
    Which is material,
    Is the Sun that shines
    For he is the essence
    In Sat, the definite
    Reality.

3. Air and sky
    Are immaterial,
    Deathless,
    Fluid, gaseous,
    Indefinable.
    The essence of "That"
    Which is numinous
    Is the Supreme Being

Inherent in the Sun.
He is the essence of
Tyad the indefinite.
This is also true for the Gods.

4. All except breath
   And ether
   In the body is material,
   And definable.
   The essence of "That"
   Which is phenomenal
   Is the eye,
   It is the essence of
   Sat, the definite Reality.

5. Breath and ether in
   The body
   Are immaterial,
   Immortal, fluid, gaseous,
   Indefinable.
   The essence of "That" which
   Is numinous
   Is the Supreme Being,
   In the right eye,
   "That" is the essence of
   The indefinite.

6. How does the Supreme Being appear
   In a vision of a saffron-coloured robe,
   Soft as wool,
   Fringed by the brilliant purple of
   Cochineal,[56]
   The flame of fire
   As gracious as the white
   Lotus,
   As sudden as the
   Lightning flash.
   Now follows the Brahmanic
   Teaching by No, No,[57]
   There is nothing higher
   Than saying it is not so, not so,
   Then is revealed what remains,
   The True of the Truth,
   The senses being the Truth
   And Brahman the Truth of
   Them all.

Part 4

1. When Yagnavalkya
   Was about to visit another
   Part of the country,
   He said to Maitreyi his first wife,
   "Truly I am leaving my house

> And going to dwell in the
> Forest as a Sannyasin,
> So let me make some
> Arrangements for you
> And my second wife Katyayam."

Yagnavalkya is a great sage renowned in the Upanishads, as was King Janaka. The "second wife" was common in Vedic times. The first wife bore the children and mastered the family. The second wife was younger and accepted by the family as an intellectual and recreational companion for the husband when the first wife was ageing. Some scholars suggest that Yagnavalkya's first wife had died and he then remarried. The question has never been finally determined.

2. Maitreyi answered,
    "My Lord, if this whole world
    Full of wealth belonged to me
    Would I be Immortal as a result?"
    "No!" replied Yagnavalkya,
    "You would be then living
    The life that rich people live.
    There is no hope whatsoever
    Of Immortality through wealth."[58]

3.   Maitreyi said, "What
     Should I do with anything
     That will not lead to Immortality?
     Please, my Lord and husband,
     Teach me about a way to Immortality."

4.   Yagnavalkya answered sweetly,
     "You who are truly very dear to me
     Speak so wisely.
     Sit down here and I will tell you,
     But mark well what I say.

5.   Truly a husband is not dear
     That you may merely love
     Him as husband,
     But it is for the love
     Of the Self of Consciousness
     That a husband is dearly loved.
     Truly sons are not dear
     That you may love the sons,
     But that you may love
     The Self of Consciousness
     Therefore sons are dear.
     Truly wealth is not dear
     That you may love wealth,
     But that you may love
     The Self of Consciousness

Therefore wealth is dear.
Truly the Brahmin Caste is not dear
That you may love
The Brahmin Caste,
But that you may love
The Self of Consciousness
Therefore the Brahmin Caste is dear.
Truly the Warrior Caste is not dear
That you may love
The Warrior Caste,
But that you may love
The Self of Consciousness
Therefore the Warrior Caste is dear.
Truly the worlds are not dear
That you may love
The Worlds,
But that you may love
The Self of Consciousness
Therefore the worlds are dear.
Truly the Gods are not dear
That you may love the Gods,
But that you may love
The Self of Consciousness
Therefore the Gods are dear.
Truly, creatures are not dear
That you love creatures,
But that you may love the Self

Of Consciousness
Are creatures dear.
Truly everything is not dear
That you may love everything
But that you may love
The Self of Consciousness,
Everything is dear.
Truly the Self of Consciousness
Is to be seen,
Heard,
Perceived,
Noted
Oh Maitreyi!
When we see
Hear
Perceive
Know
The Self of Consciousness
Then all is known.

Loving the Self, one loves all because the same Consciousness imbues the all. All there is is God, God is all there is. All there is is Consciousness, Consciousness is all there is. These are the essential truths of non-duality, Advaita Vedanta.

6. Whoever looks for the Brahmin Caste
    Elsewhere than in the Self
    Of Consciousness, Awareness,
    Should be abandoned by them;
    As with the Warrior Caste,
    Worlds,
    Gods,
    Creatures,
    Everything,
    All there is is that Self of Consciousness.

7–9. Now as a drum beat
    When sounded
    Cannot be seized by the hands,
    But the sound is seized
    When the drum and beater are seized,
    As with the conch shell
    And its blower
    And the lute and the lutenist.

10. As smoke clouds arise from a fire
    Kindled with damp sticks,
    So, truly, oh Maitreyi,
    Has been breathed from Brahman,
    Consciousness,
    The Vedas, Mythologies,
    Knowledge, Upanishads,
    Verses, Grammar, and Sage Wisdom.

11. As all waters return to the sea,
     All touches to skin,
     All tastes to tongue,
     All smells to nose,
     All colours to eyes,
     All sounds to ears,
     All concepts to mind,
     All knowledge to head,
     All actions to hands,
     All movements to feet,
     And all Vedas in speech.

12. As salt dissolves in
     Water
     And cannot be taken back,
     Yet whenever we taste
     Water it is salty,
     So truly, oh Maitreyi,
     Brahman, as Consciousness, is endless, Infinite,
     Consisting of nothing
     But Knowledge,
     Organizing the elements
     And vanishing again in them.
     When Brahman leaves,
     There are no more names left, oh Maitreyi."

13.   Maitreyi spoke:
      "Here, beloved husband,
      You have bewildered me.
      When you say that 'having departed'
      Knowledge ceases."
      Yagnavalkya answered,
      "Oh wife, I say nothing bewildering.
      This is sufficient, oh beloved,
      For understanding Wisdom.
      For if there is one whiff of duality left,
      One sees,
      Smells,
      Hears,
      Salutes,
      Perceives,
      Knows
      The other.
      But when the Self, Consciousness,
      Awareness, Reality, Brahman,
      Only is all 'That',
      How could he or she smell,
      See,
      Hear,
      Salute,
      Perceive,
      Know another?
      How should he know 'That'

By whom he knows all 'That Is'?
How, oh beloved, should he know
His or her own Self, The Knower?"

This important verse acknowledges women, as does Ramana
Maharshi, as being equal with men for Self-Realization. Were
not Ananda Maya, Mirabai, Aurobindo's mother, Ammaji, and
Mira Pagal enlightened? Of course they were and are. In
addition the verse ends duality and leads into Advaita – all
there is is Brahman, Brahman is all there is! When non-duality
is understood then there are "no others". Others are an
appearance, but as instruments of the divine they are
Consciousness imbued with form, as we all are.

Part 5

The Upanishad opens with a philosophical poem around the
metaphor of honey.[59]

1. This Earth is sweet honey,
    Waxed by all beings
    And all beings are hard working
    Honey bees of this Earth.
    This right Immortal Supreme Being
    In this Earth and in the body
    Is the same as Self, the deathless
    Consciousness, Reality, Love, Brahman,
    "That" is the All.

2. The waters are honey
    Of all beings,
    All beings are honey
    Of waters.
    This bright, deathless Supreme
    Being in the waters,
    And that existing as seed
    In the body,
    Is the same as "That"
    Immortal Self of Consciousness,
    Awareness, Brahman, the All.

3. This fire is honey
    Of all beings,
    All beings are honey
    Of this fire.
    The bright deathless
    Supreme Being in the fire,
    And that existing as speech
    In the body,
    Is the same as "That"
    Immortal Self of Consciousness,
    Awareness, Brahman, the All.

4. Air is the honey
    Of all beings,
    All beings are the honey of air.
    That bright deathless

Supreme Being in air
And the breath in body
Are the same as "That" Self,
Immortal, Consciousness, Reality, Love
Brahman, the All.

5. The Sun is honey
Of all beings,
All beings are honey
Of this Sun.
That shining deathless
Supreme Being in this Sun,
And that shining eye in the body
Are the same as "That"
Self, Immortal, Consciousness,
Reality, Love, Brahman, the All.

6. Space is honey
Of all beings,
All beings are honey
Of space.
The bright deathless
Supreme Being in space,
The same as that bright immortal ear
In the body,
"That" is the same as the deathless
Self of Consciousness, Reality, Love,
Brahman, the All.

[251]

7. The cool light of the gracious Moon
   Is indeed honey of all beings,
   And all beings are honey of Moon.
   The bright deathless
   Supreme Being inherent in Moon,
   And "That" as mind
   In the body of man,
   Are the same as "That" Self
   Of Consciousness, Reality, Love,
   Brahman, the All.

8. Lightning is the honey of all
   Beings,
   All beings are honey of lightning.
   The bright deathless
   Supreme Being in a lightning flash,
   And "That" which is light in the body
   Is the same as "That" deathless
   Self of Consciousness, Reality, Love,
   Brahman, the All.

9. Thunder is honey,[60]
   Of all beings,
   All beings are honey
   Of the thunderclap.
   This bright Supreme Being
   In this sound,

And that as voice
In the body, are the same
As "That" deathless Self of Consciousness,
Reality, Love,
Brahman, the All.

10. Ether is honey
Of all beings,
All beings are
The honey of ether.
This bright deathless
Supreme Being in ether,
And as Heart-ether
In the body,
"That" indeed is the
Same as "That" Self
Of Consciousness, Reality, Love,
Deathless,
Brahman, the All.

11. The Law of Righteousness[61]
Is the honey of all beings,
All beings are honey
Of this Law.
"That" bright deathless Supreme Being in Law,
And that righteousness inherent
In the body are the same.

That indeed is "That"
Deathless Self of Consciousness,
Reality, Love, Brahman, the All.

12. This Truth is honey
    For all beings,
    All beings are honey
    Of this Truth.
    The bright deathless Supreme Being in the Truth,
    And the same Truth inherent in mankind are
    One.
    "That" indeed is the same
    As "That" deathless Self
    Of Consciousness, Reality, Love,
    Brahman, the All.

13. Mankind is honey of all creatures,
    All creatures are honey of mankind.
    That bright Immortal Supreme Being,
    Existing as man in the body,
    Is as that deathless Self
    Of Consciousness, Reality, God, Love, Peace,
    "That" Brahman, the All.

14. This Self of Consciousness, Awareness, Love,
    Is the honey of all beings,
    All beings are honey of the Self.
    This bright Immortal Supreme Person in

"That" Self
And "That" Consciousness of both
Are an offering of honey to the Self,
All are indeed the same as "That",
Self, Immortal, Reality,
Brahman, Love, the All.

15. Truly "That" Self of Consciousness,
Reality, is the Lord of all beings,
The King of All.
And as all spokes are
Held in the axle and felly
Of a wheel,
All beings and all those sieves
Of the elements,
Earth, air, fire and water,
Are held in the Self
Of Consciousness, Reality, Love, Brahman.

19b. Hearing all this Upanishad
A sage said, "Brahman as Consciousness
Conformed himself to every form,
This is the One form of 'That'
For all to know.
By his magic powers of Maya
Does Indra travel in many a form,
Yoked are his thousand steeds."

Verses 16–19a are omitted by many translators in their abridgements as they are mythological, concerning the Asvins (the twin physician gods). It relates how they were taught this "Madhu-Vidya", the knowledge of honey, by Dadhyak Atharrana through the head of a horse.

THE CHANDOGYA
UPANISHAD

Introduction

This is a very long and important Upanishad which belongs to
the Sama Veda. Chandogya is the renowned singer poet of the
Sama Vedic Hymns — the cream of the Vedas, famed for their
musicality. Shankara made an extensive commentary.[62] I have
had to make an abridgement on traditional lines.

BOOK I

Part 1

1. Meditate on the sacred syllable
    AUM.

2. AUM
    The essence of all being is Earth,
    Of Earth, water,
    Of water, plants,
    Of plants, man,
    Of man, speech,

Of speech, the Rig Veda,
Of the Rig Veda, the Sama Veda,
Of the Sama Veda, the Udigatha.
AUM.

3. "That" AUM is the best
   Of all essences,
   The highest,
   Worthy of the Supreme Place,
   The Eighth.

4. What is the Rik?
   What is the Saman?
   What is the Udigatha?

5. Rik is speech,
   Saman is breath,
   Udigatha is AUM.
   All speech, breath,
   Rik and Saman
   Form one couple.

6. That couple is linked
   In AUM.
   When man and woman come together
   They fulfil their highest desires.

7. He who knows "That"
   Meditates on AUM,
   A fulfiller of highest desires.

8. AUM is the syllable
   Of acceptance,
   Whenever we welcome
   We chant AUM, yea
   Affirmation is gratification.
   He who knows "That"
   Meditates on AUM
   And becomes a gratifier
   Of "what is"
   And is freed from misery.

9. By AUM does
   The threefold knowledge move.
   When the Priest officiates
   He chants AUM,
   As do the Hotri and
   Udgatri Priests,
   All for its glory.

10. Knowledge and ignorance
    Are different,
    The sacrifice which a man
    Or woman

Performs with knowledge,
Faith and this Upanishad
Is more powerful.
"That" is AUM.

Part 2

Verses 1–6 discuss the war between gods and devils. The gods
revere AUM, the devils corrupt the meaning.

7. Then comes the oral Life Breath,
   The Gods meditate on AUM
   As "That" breath.
   When the devils touched "That"
   They were shattered
   As a ball of earth
   When it hits rock.

8. In the same way
   He or she who wishes evil,
   Or persecutes
   Anyone who knows "That"
   Will be shattered
   For he or she is a strong stone.

9. By the mouth breath he discerns
    Whether there is good or bad intent.
    Bad smelling breath points to evil,
    Pure breath points to virtue.
    What we eat and drink
    Supports the life forces in the senses.
    On leaving the body
    He fails to find that oral breath
    Through which he eats, drinks
    And lives. He dies.
    At the time of death he drops the jaw
    As if to eat.

Verses 10–14 are omitted in abridgements as they record
different rishis' meditations on the above verses, which are
largely repetitive.

Part 3

1. Here is the meditation on
    AUM
    By the Gods.
    Let a man or woman meditate
    On AUM
    As he or she who sends warmth like the Sun.
    When the Sun dawns it chants
    AUM for all beings,

It destroys darkness and fear.
He who knows "That"
Destroys ignorance.

2.   So the oral Life Breath
     And "That" of the Sun
     Are the same.
     Both are warm,
     One is called sound
     The other, reflected sound.
     So let a man or woman
     Meditate on AUM
     As breath and Sun.

The rest of this part, as well as 4–8 that explain detailed
technicalities of the sacred chant, are omitted as in many
abridgements.

Part 9

1.   "What is the origin of the world?"
     Said Silaka.
     "Consciousness," said Pravahana.
     "From Consciousness all beings
     Arise.
     'That' is the substratum.
     They return to Consciousness.

Consciousness precedes being,
Consciousness is also there at Death.

2. Consciousness is indeed
    AUM-Brahman,
    Greater than the greatest without end.
    He or she who understands 'That'
    Meditates on AUM
    He or she conquers all worlds."

3. Saunaka having taught
    AUM to Udara said,
    "As long as your family
    Knows this AUM
    Their life in the world
    Will be greater than great."

Parts 10 and 11 are omitted. They tell the story of Ushasti, a mendicant, called upon to perform the Vedic sacrifice. They are largely repetitive verses.

Part 12 gives the chant of dogs and magical correlations between sounds and phenomena, as does Book II, Parts 1–22.

BOOK II

Part 23

In this chapter, I have transcreated the parts as separate poems rather than breaking the flow by numerated verses, and I have done the same in Book III.

> There are three branches
> Of the righteous way,[63]
> Sacrifice,
> Study,
> Charity, first,
> Austerity, next,
> To dwell as a Brahmin Pupil
> In the house of a Teacher is third.
> All three reach the worlds of the blest.
> But he or she firmly
> Grounded in Brahman
> Is Immortal.
> The Primeval Father
> Brooded
> And AUM was born.
> As all leaves have a stalk
> So are all words linked to AUM,
> AUM is all This, yes
> AUM is all "That".

Part 24 on the rewards of sacrifice is not transcreated.

BOOK III

Parts 1–10 relating how the sun is seen as honey, extracted from the Vedas, is left out.

Part 11

When the Sun dawns
He neither rises nor sets,
He is alone,
Centred,
To he or she who knows,
In this secret doctrine of the Veda,
There is neither rising nor setting
There is only day,
Once and for all.
A father may tell
This to his eldest son
Or a worthy pupil,
But no one should
Tell it to anybody
Even if offered a whole world
Of treasure.
This teaching
Is worth more than "That"
Yes worth very much more.

Part 12

The Gayatri[64] verse is
Everything that exists,
It is speech,
It sings forth
And guards all.
It is the Earth,
The body,
The vital airs,
The Heart,
The senses.
It has four metric feet
And is sixfold.
Such is the greatness
Of Brahman metrically
Disguised as Gayatri.

Compare the following from the Rig Veda III. 62:10:

Let us adore the supremacy
Of that divine Sun,
The Godhead
Who illuminates all,
From whom all proceed,
To whom all must
Return,

Whom we invoke
To direct our understandings
Aright in our progress
Towards his sacred state
Of Self-Realization.
We meditate
On the divine light
Of Savitri,
The Sun God,
May it enlighten
Our intellectual understanding.

This is one form of the Gayatri Mantra, which is translated in many ways. An alternative fuller translation is:

Through the coming and going
Of the balance of existence
The True Nature which illumines Life
As the Sun,
Is beloved,
May all mankind through their subtle intellect
Reach the brilliance of enlightenment.
Greater than the soul[65]
His feet are
All Immortal,
Three feet in heaven,
Its own Self

Of Consciousness, Reality, Love.
It is as the ether
Within and without,
In the Heart,
As Brahman,
Omnipresent,
Immutable.
He who knows "That"
Is truly content.

Part 13

Part 13, 1–6 on the vital breaths is left out.

7. That light
   Shining above heaven,
   Higher than all,
   Is the highest world,
   That is the same light
   Immanent in men and women,
   We can have visible proof.[66]
   We know by touch,
   Heat is the body,
   If we stop the ears
   We hear rolling of chariots,
   Bellowing of oxen
   Or burning fires.

Let a man or woman
Meditate on "That"
As Brahman, seen and heard.
He who knows "That"
Becomes famed and celebrated.

Part 14

All "That" is Brahman,
Let a man meditate
On the world of appearance,
The visible as beginning, ending,
Breathing in "That".
Men and women are creatures of will.[67]
As his or her will is
So shall he or she be when leaving the body,
So have this will and belief.
The intelligent whose body is spirit,
Whose form is light,
Whose thoughts are truth,
Natural, ethereal,
Omnipresent,
Invisible.
From whom all worlds,
Desires,
Fragrances,
Tastes proceed,

He or she who warmly embraces
All "That"
Who is silent, calm
"That" is my Self of Consciousness,
Within the Heart,
Smaller than a barley corn,
A mustard seed,[68]
A canary seed,
Or even its kernel.
He is also my Self of Consciousness
Within the Heart,
Space to contain the Earth,
The sky,
The heavens
And all worlds.
That from whom all worlds,
All desires,
All fragrances, tastes,
Who warmly embraces all
"That"
Who is silent, calm
"That" is my Self of Consciousness
Within the Heart, Brahman.
When I leave the body
I shall reach that same Self,
The Source of Consciousness.
He who holds this strong faith

Is doubt free.
So spoke Sandilya,
Yes, he spoke that way!

Part 15, which is about taking refuge in various gods, and 16,
a vision of life seen as a soma sacrifice, are not included in this
abridgement. Part 17 is also omitted as it is mainly concerned
with procedures of the sacrificial rites.

Part 18

Let men and women
Meditate on mind in body
As Brahman,
And the ether in the Gods.
So both meditations
On body-mind
And the Gods
Are taught.
Brahman as mind
Has four feet,
Speech,
Breath,
Eye,
Ear.
Brahman as Gods
Also has four feet,

Agni, fire;
Vayu, air;
Aditya, Sun;
And all encompassing space.
So both the worship
Which is of mind-body
And "That" which belongs
To the Gods is taught.
Speech is the first foot of Brahman
"That" shines with fire as its light
And radiantly heats.
He who knows "That" shines and warms
Through his celebrated fame
And glorious face.
Breath is the second foot
"That" shines with air
As its light and warms.
He who knows "That"
Brilliantly shines and glows
Through his celebrated fame
And glorious face.
The eye is the third foot of Brahman
"That" shines with the Sun
As it lights and heats.
He who knows "That"
Shines dazzlingly and warms
Through his celebrated fame

And glorious face.
The ear is the fourth foot
"That" shines
With the all encompassing space
As it lights and heats.
He who knows "That" glows and warms
Through his celebrated fame
And glorious face.

Part 19 is omitted as it is a far-fetched analogy of the sun as an egg.

BOOK IV

Parts 1 and 2 are omitted. They are the story of Janasruiti, an "untouchable", or Sudra of lower caste who has become wealthy as a restauranteur. He built many guest houses. It is a literary diversion and discusses gambling with dice. He discovers a sage called Raskva, who gives his teaching in Part 3. Gambling with dice was a popular recreation in Vedic times – and was a cause of the quarrel which caused the war in which Arjuna asked for Krishna's advice and hence the Bhagavad Gita!

Part 3

1. Air is the end of all,
   For when fire dies,
   When the Sun sets,
   When the Moon goes down,
   It is in air that all merges.

2. When water dries up
   Air consumes them all,
   "That" is for the Gods.

3. This is for the body,
   Breath is the end of all,
   When a man or woman's
   Sleep,

Speech,
Sight,
Hearing,
Mind,
All are consumed by breath.

The rest of this chapter is 4–8, the story of Jaunake and Atipratorin, who while dining were visited by a beggar. They refused to give him alms. He was a student of Brahman. He discourses to them, they give him food, and it ends with a meditation on food from a Vedic standpoint.

From Part 4 to Part 14 there is a series of anecdotal stories illustrating many points of Vedic teaching. As this is a traditional abridgement, these tales are omitted and resume at verses central to the core of the Upanishad.

Part 15

1. The Teacher of Satyakama
   Said, "The Supreme Being[69] seen in the eye,
   That is Self, Immortal,
   Fearless Brahman.
   Even though they drop
   Hot melted butter on 'That'
   Or oceans of water on 'That'
   It falls away on both sides.

2. They call him Blessed
   For all blessings go
   Towards him.
   Who knows 'That'.

3. He leads all blessings,
   He shines in all worlds,
   Who knows 'That'.

4. Now if one who knows
   'That' dies,
   He goes to light,
   From light to day,
   By day to the bright half of the Moon,
   Then to the waxing six months of the Sun,
   To the year,
   To the Sun,
   To the Moon,
   To the lightning,
   There is a Supreme Being – Inhuman.

5. He leads them to 'That'
   Brahman, Consciousness,
   This is the way of the Gods.
   Those who take this path
   Do not return to the world."

Parts 16 and 17 are aspects of the sacrifice and are omitted.

BOOK V

Parts 1 and 2 are left out as they are almost identical with the Brihadaranyaka Upanishad VI, Parts 1 and 2. Part 3 is also a repetition but it has significant differences, so it is included, as another version.

Part 3

1. Svetaketu went to a meeting
   Of the Pankalas.
   King Pravahana said to him,
   "My boy, has your father
   Taught you well?"
   "Yes," he answered.

2. "Do you know to what place
   Men go from here?"
   "No," he replied.
   "Do you know how they come
   Back?"
   "No."
   "Do you know where the path
   Of Gods and the Ancestors
   Diverge?"
   "No."
   "Do you know why the world

Of the Ancestors
Never becomes full?"
"No."
"Do you know why in the fifth
Libation
Water has a human voice?"
"No."
"Then why say you had been well taught?
Your ignorance betrays the fact
You have not been well taught."
Saddened, the boy went
To his father and said,
"You have not instructed me well
Although you say you have.
King Pravahana asked me five questions.
I could not answer one!"
His father said,
"I do not know answers
To these questions,
If I did, I would have told you."
So Gautama went to see the King.
The King said, "Ask me for a boon."
"Tell me what you said to the boy."
The King was perplexed and said,
"Stay here with me,
This knowledge never was
Told to any Brahmin.

It belongs to the Warrior class alone."
Then he began.

Part 4

1. "The altar is heaven,
   Gautama,
   Its fuel is the Sun,
   The smoke its rays,
   The light the day,
   The coals the Moon,
   The stars the sparks.

2. On that altar
   The Gods
   Led by Agni
   Offer the libation of water.
   From 'That' arises Soma
   The ecstatic nature,
   The King of Plants,
   Gracious moonlight.

Part 5

The altar is the God of Rain,
Its fuel is air,
The smoke the cloud,
The light the lightning flash,

The coals the thunderbolt,
The sparks the thunderclaps.
On that altar the Gods offer Soma
The ecstatic nature,
The King of Plants, gracious moonlight.
From that offering comes rainfall.

Part 6

The altar is the Earth,
Its fuel the year,
The smoke the ether,
The light the night,
The coals the corner of space,
The sparks the space between.
On that altar the Gods offer rain,
From that offering arises food,
Corn and the harvests.

Part 7

The altar is man,
Its fuel is speech,
The smoke the breath,
The light the tongue,
The coals the eye,
The sparks the ear.

On that altar the Gods offer corn,
From that offering
Springs forth seed.

Part 8

Woman is the fire,
The phallus her fuel,
When the husband approaches
This is her smoke,
The vulva is her flame,
When the husband enters
This is her coal,
Her sparks are ecstasy.
In this fire the Gods offer semen,
From this offering comes the embryo.

Part 9

1. So water is the fifth offering
Called mankind,
This embryo, warmed
In the womb
For nine to ten months
Is then born.

2. When born,
   He or she lives
   A predestined time,
   When he or she leaves the body
   His friends take him or her
   To the funeral fire
   From where he or she emerged
   Initially.

Part 10

1. Those who know
   This teaching of the five fires,
   Even though they are householders,
   And those forest Rishis
   Who follow faith and austerities,
   And those Yogis who can leave the body
   And enter into another, at will,
   And those who do not yet know
   The Highest Brahman
   As Consciousness, Reality, Peace,
   Still go to light,
   From light to day,
   From day to the half Moon,
   To the six months when the Sun waxes
   From the year, to the Sun,
   From the Sun, to the full Moon,

And then to lightning flash.
There is a Supreme Person,
Inhuman.

2. 'That' leads them to Brahman,
   The perceivable Brahman,
   This is the way of the Gods.

3. But they who dwell
   In a village
   Only live a life of austerities
   And good works,
   They ascend to smoke,
   Smoke to night,
   From night to dark half of Moon,
   To the six months
   When the Sun wanes,
   They do not reach the year.

4. From months they go
   To the world of the Ancestors,
   From the Ancestors
   To the ether,
   From ether to full Moon,
   That is Soma,
   The royal plant of natural ecstasy,
   Here they are eaten by the Gods,
   Yes the Gods enjoy them.

5. Having dwelled there
    Until these noble works
    Are consumed,
    They return again
    As they came
    To the ether,
    From ether to air,
    Then the sacrificer becomes air,
    Becomes smoke and then mist.

6. Having become mist,
    He or she becomes a cloud
    And then rains down.
    Then he or she is born as rice,
    Corn,
    Herbs,
    Trees,
    Sesame,
    Beans,
    Then escape is hard,
    Whenever persons eat food
    And have children
    He or she becomes as one of them.

7. Those of noble conduct
    Soon attain good birth,
    As a Brahmin,
    Warrior

Or Merchant,
But those of wicked conduct
Reach an evil birth,
Dog, hog,
Or social outcast.

8. On either of these paths
Are insects like flies
Or reptiles like worms,
Always coming back,
They live and die
So the world never becomes full.
So let a man take care.

9. A man who steals gold,
Drinks spirits,
Dishonours the bed of his guru,
Who kills a Brahmin,
These four fall and those
Who mix with them.

10. Yet he who knows the five fires
Is undefiled even if he mixes with them.
He who knows this teaching is pure and clean
And reaches the world of the blest."

Part 11

1. Eight great householders,
    Aupamanyara, Satyayagna,
    Paulushi, Indradyumna,
    Bhallaveya, Gana, Sarkarakekya,
    And Asvatarasvi,
    Who were also theologians,
    Once met to discuss
    The Nature of the Self and Brahman.

2. They pondered and agreed,
    "There is one Aruni
    Who knows the Self."
    They decided to call on him.

3. But Aruni hesitated.
    "These householders and theologians
    Will cross-examine me,
    I cannot tell them all I know
    So I will suggest someone else."

4. He said, "Sirs, King Kaikeya
    Knows the Self,"
    So they went to see him.

5.   When they arrived
   The King gave them gifts
   And in the morning announced,
   "In my kingdom
   There is no thief,
   Miser,
   Drunkard,
   Atheist,
   Ignoramus,
   Adulterer
   Or
   Adulteress.
   I shall perform a sacrifice,
   And as much wealth
   As I give
   To each Rig Veda Priest,
   I shall give to you,
   Please stay."

6.   They answered, "Everyone
   Will say why he comes,
   You know the Self, tell us all."

7.   The King replied, "Tomorrow
   I shall tell you."
   On the next morning they came
   Bearing fuel, like students,

But the King without demanding rites
Satisfied with their humility, spoke.

Part 12

1. "Now Aupamanyara,
Whom do you meditate on as Self?"
He answered, "Only heaven,
Your Majesty."
"Ah," said the King,
"That Self you meditate on is
The Vaisvanara Self[70]
The sum total of all created
Beings in the Universe,
You meditate on Brahman,
Taking bodily fire
As a symbol
Instead of Virat, the world
Which appears to us.
This is a good insight.
So every kind of Soma libation,
The divine plant
Of Royal Ecstasy,
Is found in your house.

2. You eat food and witness
   Your desires
   Maybe for a son or daughter?
   Whoever so meditates
   On 'That' Vaisvanara Self
   Eats food, witnesses his desires
   And enjoys Vedic glory
   Arising from study
   And austerity in his home.
   'That' is only the head
   Of the Self.
   Your head would have
   Fallen off
   In discussion
   If God had not brought you here."

Part 13

1. Then the King addressed
   Satyayagna and asked
   Him, "Whom do you meditate
   On as Self?"
   He answered, "The Sun only, your Majesty."
   The King answered, "The Self
   You meditate on is
   Also the Vaisvanara Self,
   The multiform,

So vast wealth is seen
In your home.

2.   You have an estate
Full of slaves, mules and jewels,
You enjoy and witness your desires,
Whoever meditates so
Has Vedic Glory in his home.
That however is only the eye of Self
And you would have become blind
If you did not come here."

Part 14

Then the King spoke to Indradyumna
And asked him, "On what do you
Meditate as Self?"
"Air only," he replied.
The King answered, "The Self
You meditate on is also the Vaisvanara,
So gifts come to you unsought,
Rows of chariots follow you around.
You eat food and witness your desires,
Whomever meditates on this
Has Vedic Glory in his home,
But this is only the breath of Self
And your breath would have
Left you if you had not come here!"

Part 15

1. Then he said to Gana,
   "Whom do you meditate on as Self?"
   He answered, "Ether, your Majesty."
   He replied, "The Self which you
   Meditate on is also the Vaisvanara
   Self called fullness.
   So you are filled with family relations
   And wealth.

2. You eat food and witness
   Your desires,
   And whoever meditates
   Like that has Vedic Glory in his home.
   That however is but the trunk of the Self,
   Your trunk would have died
   If you had not come here."

Part 16

1. Then he said to Bhallaveya,
   "Whom do you meditate
   On as Self?"
   "Water only, your Majesty."
   The King replied, "The Self
   On which you meditate

Is also the Vaisvanara Self
Called wealth.
So you are very rich
And prosperous.

2.   You eat food and witness
     Your desires,
     Whoever meditates on that Self
     Has Vedic Glory in his house.
     That however is only the feet
     Of the Self and your feet
     Would have collapsed
     If you had not come here."

Part 17

1.   Then the King said to them all,
     "Now listen, all of you, eat your food
     Knowing that Self as manifold,
     Yet he who worships
     The Self as Pure Consciousness
     And as identical with himself!
     He will enjoy good food
     In all worlds,
     With all beings,
     With all Selves,
     Of that Self the head is light,

The eye multiform,
The breath spacious, the trunk full,
The bladder wealth,
The feet the Earth, chest the altar,
Hairs the sacred altar grass,
The Heart, mind and speech
The fire!"

Chapters 18 to 24 are concerned with the minutiae of various offerings, sacrifices and oblations and they are omitted in this abridgement.

BOOK VI

Part 1

Harihi AUM.

1. Once there lived a certain Svetaketu.
   One day his father told him to attend Vedic school:
   "As there is no one belonging to our family
   Who not having studied Brahman
   Was a Brahmin only by birth."

2. At twelve years old
   He started with a teacher
   And came home again
   When he was twenty-four
   Having studied all the Vedas.
   He was puffed up and pompous
   Waggling his plumes,
   Believing he was erudite
   And somewhat severe,
   Living in only his head.

3. His Father said,
   "Oh, Svetaketu,
   You are so conceited and stern,
   Have you asked for that teaching

By which we hear
What cannot be heard,
By which we perceive
What cannot be perceived,
By which we know
What cannot be known?"

4. "What is that teaching?"
    He replied.
    His Father answered,
    "My dear son,
    As by one clod of clay
    All that is made of clay is known,
    The difference being only a name
    Arising from speech,
    But the truth being all is clay!
    The same is true for all made of gold
    And by one pair of nail scissors all iron is
    Known."
    The son said,
    "Surely my revered teachers
    Did not know that
    Or they would have told me."
    "Be it so, my son.

Part 2

1. In the beginning, my son,
   There was 'That',
   Only 'what is',
   Consciousness,
   One without a second.
   Others say in the beginning
   There was only 'That',
   'What is not'
   And from 'That' came 'That'
   'What is'.

2. But this is impossible, my boy,
   How could 'That' 'what is'
   Be born from 'That'
   'What is not'?
   No, my dear, only 'That'
   'What is'
   Was in the beginning
   One only, Consciousness,
   Without a second.

3. Consciousness brooded,
   'May I be many,
   May I increase,'
   It sent forth fire.

That fire pondered,
'May I also be many,
May I increase,' it sent forth water.
And so whenever anybody is overheated
He sweats water.
Water too thought,
'May I be many, may I increase,'
It sent forth food.
So whenever it rains, crops flower,
From water comes our sustenance.

Part 3

1. There are two origins
   Of all living beings
   Born of an egg,
   Oviparous,
   Or from a living germ,
   Viviparous.

2. 'That' which had made fire, water, earth, air,
   Elementally brooded
   And entered them with 'That',
   Consciousness, Atman, Self,
   And then made these archetypes
   Manifest as manifold names and forms.

3. Then 'That' having made
    An admixture of these elements
    Many diverse objects were formed,
    Named, and manifested.

4. I shall inform you how
    Consciousness executed this feat.

Part 4

1. The red of Agni
    Is the colour of fire,
    The white water,
    The black of Earth,
    So disappears what we call 'fire',
    Just a word from speech.

2. What is left and true
    Are the colours
    Red, black, and white.

3. The reddish tone of the late Moon
    Is the colour of fire,
    The white of water tumbling over rocks,
    The blackness of rich soil.
    So disappears what we call Moon,
    A mere word arising

From speech.
What is true are the three colours.

The rishis developed a rather crude physics based on metaphysical insights. Colour theory, as demonstrated by Newton and progressed by Goethe and Schopenhauer, shows that colour recognition is "a priori" in the organ of cognition, the brain and retina, e.g. for a colour-blind man there is no colour. This Upanishad may be pointing at an essence that creates the illusion of colour. Nature is painted by light in innumerable tones and hues, as Newton discovered. Redness, for example, is all of the spectrum absorbed except for the redness which is reflected back to the brain of the observer, where it is congruent with or corresponds with redness in the organ of cognition, brain and senses.

4. The red of the lightning
   Flash is fire,
   The rush of the waterfall
   Is white,
   The rich ploughed soil
   Is black.
   So ends what we name
   Lightning,
   A mere figure of speech.
   The colours are real.

5. Ancient householders
    And theologians
    Who knew this emanation
    From these three colours
    Said, 'We know all.'

It is possible the Upanishad is pointing to the three *gunas* or
states, which make up all natural phenomena with the
juxtaposition of the elements. Red is *rajas*, the active force;
white, the *sattva* neutralizing force; *tamas*, the black force of
passive inertia.

6. What appears as red
    They saw as fire,
    The white indicated
    Water,
    The black they saw
    As Earth.

The air is transparent; like Consciousness it has no apparent
colour but reflects the colour that appears on its screen,
mentally interpreted.

7. Whatever was thought
    To be unknown
    They knew was
    A combination of these divine colours.

Part 5

1. Food when eaten becomes
   Threefold,
   Its gross form is shit,
   Its middle, flesh,
   Its subtlest, mind.

2. Water when drunk becomes
   Triple too,
   Its grossest is piss,
   Its middle, blood,
   Its subtlest, breath.

3. Fire in oil, butter, and so on
   Are also triple.
   Its grossest is bone,
   Its middle, marrow,
   Its subtlest, speech.
   Truly, my child,
   Mind comes from Earth,
   Breath from water,
   Speech from fire."
   "Please tell me more, Father."
   "So be it, my son.

Part 6

1. The subtle part of churned curds
    Rises up and becomes butter.
    The subtle part of food when eaten
    Rises up and becomes mind.
    The subtle part of water
    When drunk
    Rises up and becomes breath.
    The subtle part of fire
    When consumed
    Rises up and becomes speech."

2. "Please tell me more."
    "Yes, my son.

Part 7

1. Man and woman consist
    Of sixteen parts,
    Fast for fifteen days
    And drink water,
    Breath comes from water
    So you will not die."

2. Svetaketu fasted
   For fifteen days
   Then asked his Father,
   "What shall I say now to test this point?"
   He replied, "Repeat
   The Rig, Sama and Yajur Vedas."
   "I do not know them that well."

3. "As in a great bonfire,
   One tiny coal
   The size of a firefly
   May be left,
   So, my son, one sixteenth part
   Of you was left
   And with that one part
   You do not know the Vedas.
   So go and eat you must be very hungry."

4. So the boy ate
   And told his Father
   That he knew all by heart.
   The Father said,

5. "As a great bonfire,
   One coal the size
   Of a firefly
   If left may be made to blaze

By feeding it with dry grass,
And there will be a conflagration

6. So, my dear one,
   One part of your sixteenth part
   Was set on fire by food
   And now you know the Vedas."
   So the boy understood
   All his Father had taught him,
   Mind comes from food,
   Breath from water,
   Speech from fire.

Part 8

1. Aruni said to Svetaketu:
   "I will teach you the true
   Nature of sleep.
   When a man sleeps deeply
   He is united with Brahman, pure Consciousness,
   He has gone to his own true Self,
   So they say he 'sleeps well'
   Because he has gone to his own.

2. As a parrot when tied by a string to its perch
   Flies first in every direction
   But finding no rest anywhere
   Settles down where it is fastened,

So the mind, the restless will,
After flying in every direction
Finding no rest anywhere
Settles down on the Life Breath
For, my son, the restless
Wandering, perverted mind
Is fastened to the Life Breath.

Ramana Maharshi advocated watching the flow of breath without interference as a way to quieten the mind, as the bundle of thoughts (mind) and breath come from the same source.

3. Now what are hunger and thirst?
    When a man is 'hungry'
    Water is used to digest his food
    So as there is a cowherd,
    A horse trainer, a manager,
    So water is the food leader,
    So he by food knows this body
    Could not be without a cause.

4. Where else could its cause
    Be, but in Earth?
    So as food and Earth are an offshoot
    Seek after their root that is water.
    And from fire came water,

And fire from Brahman.
Yes all these Creations
Are rooted and grounded in Brahman.
They dwell in 'That'
They rest in 'That'.

5. When a man is thirsty
Fire has carried away his drinks,
So as there is a cowherd,
A horse trainer, a manager,
So is fire, water leader.
So water absorbed
Knows this body to be born,
This body could not be
Without a cause.

6. Where is the root
Except in water?
As water is an offshoot
Seek the cause that is fire.
As fire is an adjunct, seek its root,
Its cause is Brahman.
Yes, all these Creations
Have their ground in Brahman.
They live in 'That'
They rest in 'That'.
And how these three Divine Creations,

Fire, Water, Earth,
When they reach mankind become
When a man or woman leaves the b
His speech is merged in his mind-brain,
His mind-brain in his breath,
His breath in the heat of fire,
Heat of fire in Brahman, Consciousness.

7. Now 'That' which is
   The subtle essence,
   The root of all that is
   Has its Self,
   It is Brahman, Consciousness,
   And you, my son, are 'That'."
   "Please tell me more, Father."
   "So be it.

Part 9

1. As bumble bees make honey
   By gathering nectar
   From different flowers and blossoms
   They reduce the nectar to one form.

2. As the nectar lacks discrimination
   In order to say, 'I am the nectar
   Of the apple tree
   Or the rose bush.'

And so on, my son,
So all creatures
When they are merged in Consciousness,
'That' Brahman
In either deep sleep or death,
Know not that they are merged
In the One Self.

3. Whatever these creatures are,
Fearsome lion,
Hungry wolf,
Magnificent bear,
Lowly worm,
Minute midge,
Irritating mosquito,
They return to life
Again and again.

4. Now that subtle essence,
In 'That' all that lives
Has its Self, Consciousness, Brahman,
And you, my son, are 'That'."
"Please tell me more, Father."
"So be it, my boy.

Part 10

1. Look at these rivers
    They run like the Ganges to the East
    Or like the Sindhu to the West.
    They flow from sea to sea.
    The Sun lifts water
    And returns it as rain
    By cloud messengers,[71] to the oceans.
    So the rivers become the sea
    And when they are there
    They cannot know
    I am this or that river.

Part 11

1. If someone were to axe the root
    Of this great banyan tree
    It would suffer pain, bleed, yet live.
    Also if the stem or top were struck
    It would prevail,
    Pervaded by the living Self,
    Consciousness.
    The Life Force,
    That tree stands firm
    Drinking in nourishment
    From soil, Sun and air,
    It rejoices gladly.

2. But if this Life Force
    Of Selfhood
    Leaves a branch,
    Or a leaf, it withers,
    But if 'That' leaves the whole tree
    The whole tree dies.
    In the same way, my son,
    All these created beings
    When they return from Brahman,
    Consciousness, Peace,
    Do not know they have come
    Back from 'That'!
    Whatever these creatures,
    Be they roaring lion,
    Ravenous wolf,
    Wild, tusky boar,
    Humble earthworm,
    Summer mayfly,
    Microscopic midge,
    Noxious gnat,
    Dangerous mosquito,
    They return again
    And again and again.

3. 'That' which exists
    Is that subtle essence.
    In it all that lives

Has its own Self
Of Consciousness, Awareness, Reality.
It is Brahman, Love,
And you, my son, are 'That'!"
"Please, Father, tell me more."
"So be it, my son.

According to the Veda, trees are "conscious" while Buddhists hold they are "unconscious". From an Advaitic standpoint "all there is is Consciousness".

4. This animal body
Withers too and dies
When the Self of Consciousness,
Awareness departs.
But the Self is Immortal and never dies.
'That' which is subtle essence
In all that lives
Has its own Self,
It is Brahman,
It is Consciousness,
And you, my son, are 'That'!"
"Please, Father, tell me more."
"So be it, my boy.

Part 12

This important chapter is in answer to a question posed by Svetaketu to his father. "How can this universe which has the form and name of earth be produced from the Sat Consciousness Reality which is so subtle and has neither form nor name?"

1. Fetch me a fruit
   From that fig tree."
   "Here is one."
   "Now break it."
   "I have."
   "What do you see?"
   "These seeds so minute,
   Almost infinitesimal."
   "Cut one, then."
   "I have, with difficulty."
   "What do you see?"
   "Nothing, Father."

2. "My son, that subtle essence
   Which you cannot see,
   That is the very essence
   From which this great fig tree grows and lives.

3. Believe me, my boy,
    'That' which is the subtle essence
    In all that exists
    Has its Self,
    It is Brahman, Consciousness,
    Awareness, Reality, Love,
    It is the Self and you
    Are 'That'!"
    "Please tell me more."
    "So be it, son.

This reinforces the modern view of Advaitins and many quantum physicists that Consciousness is the substratum of all that exists. As Ramesh Balsekar, the Mumbai sage, puts it, "All there is is Consciousness, Consciousness is all there is."[72]

Part 13

The question put here is if Sat Consciousness Reality is the root of all that exists, why is it not perceived?

1. My boy, put this salt
    In a glass of water
    And then come and see me
    Tomorrow morning."
    "Yes, Father."
    The following day the Father said,

"Bring the salt to me
Which you put in the water."
"I cannot find it, it has dissolved."

2. "Well then taste the water.
How is it?"
"Salty, very salty."
"Taste it from the centre,
How is it?"
"Salty, very salty."
"Spoon some from the bottom.
How is it?"
"Salty, very salty."
"Now throw it away
And come and see me."

3. "Well you threw it away,
But the salt still exists forever.
Here also in our animal body
You cannot perceive
Consciousness, Reality, Love,
Yet there indeed it is,
'That' which is the subtle essence,
'That' exists in all,
Each has its own Self,
It is Brahman, Consciousness,
It is the Self and you

Are 'That'!"
"Please tell me more."
"So be it, son.

Part 14

This chapter is a beautiful parable.

1.   A certain captive
     Was led blindfold
     From the land
     Of the Gandharas[73]
     And they leave him deserted
     Where there are no humans.
     That person would turn
     To the East, North, South or West
     And shout, 'I have been brought here blindfolded,
     Woe is me!'

2.   Then a man of good will
     Hears the shout
     And taking compassion
     Removes the blindfold.
     'Go that way, my friend,
     There you will find Gandhara.'
     Having faith in his new friend
     He starts walking

In that direction.
He asks his way
From village to village.
At last with great relief
He arrives home
A freed man
In Gandhara.
So does an earnest seeker
Meet with a wise teacher
With whom he resonates
And feels peace,
To inform him about the way
To Self-Knowledge
Or liberation from the suffering
Of Divine Hypnosis.
The guru directs him
And points out the way.
The student has faith
And without delay
Grace delivers him
From identification with his mind and body
Which has caused him
So much anguish.
He is free
Like the man from Gandhara.
'That' which is the subtle essence
In all that lives

Has its own Self of Consciousness,
It is the Truth, Reality, Brahman, Love, Peace,
And you are 'That', my son."
"Please tell me more."
"So be it, my boy.

Part 15

1. If a man or woman
    Lies very ill
    His friends and relations
    Come around
    And enquire,
    'Do you recognize me?'
    As long as his speech
    Is not merged in his mind,
    His mind in breath,
    Breath in fiery heat,
    Heat in Brahman,
    He knows them.

2. But when his speech
    Has merged in mind,
    Mind in breath,
    Breath in fiery heat,
    Heat in Brahman,
    Then he does not know them.

'That' which is the subtle
Essence in it all.
Each has its Self,
It is Consciousness, Brahman,
Peace, the True, the Self,
And you, my son, are 'That'."
"Please tell me more, Father."
"So be it, my son.

Part 16

1. They bring a thief here
    Handcuffed
    And they accuse him.
    When he denies the charge
    They prepare the axe
    By heating it up.
    If he lies he is guilty.
    The test whether he is lying
    Is if he is burnt by the axe
    When he touches it,
    He is executed.

2. If he speaks the truth
    He is not burned by the axe.

3. So a man or woman
   Is not burnt
   Because they are truthful,
   So does the whole universe
   Have this Consciousness as Self.
   'That' is the Real Truth,
   'That' is the Self,
   You are 'That' Consciousness!"
   Svetaketu understood "That"
   Now, well and truly.

Justice for felony was rough and swift in those days to discourage crime at all levels, as in Medieval Europe; without police forces, strong deterrents were the only way to keep the peace.

BOOK VII

Part 1

Narada[74] approached
The sage Sanatkumara
And said, "Teach me, Sir."
Sanatkumara said, "First tell me
What you understand,
Then I will tell you what is
Beyond 'That'."
Narada said,
"I know all the Vedas,
The Rig, Yajur, Sama,
The Atharvana, the Mahabharata,
The laws of Grammar,
The rule for Sacrifice,
Mathematics,
Astrology,
The theory of Time,
Logic,
Ethics,
Etymology,
The Science[75] of Pronunciation,
Ceremony,
Prosody,
Ritual,

Demons,
Martial Arts,
Astronomy,
Poisons,
Fragrances,
Dancing,
Singing,
Playing instruments,
The Fine Arts,
All this I know well, Sir.
Also I know the Mantras,
The Sacred Books,
But alas I do not know
The Self.
I have heard from sages
That he who knows the Self
Overcomes suffering.
I am suffering,
Do Sir, help me
I implore you.
I know that he or she
Who meditates on the Name
As Brahman,
Is Lord and Master
Of 'That'
But, Sir, is there something
Better than a name?"

"Yes there is something
Better than a name."
"Please tell me, Sir."

Part 2

"Speech is better than a name,
Speech makes us understand the Vedas,
All the sciences you know
And the heavens,
Earth,
Air,
Ether,
Water,
Fire,
Gods,
Men,
Women,
Cattle,
Birds,
Herbs,
Trees,
Animals,
Reptiles,
Insects,
What is right and wrong,[76]
True and false,

Good and bad,
Pleasant and unpleasant,
For without speech
All this science
Would not be understood.
So meditate on speech.
He or she who meditates
On speech as Brahman
Becomes Lord and Master
As far as speech reaches."
"But, Sir, is there something
Beyond speech?"
"Yes."
"Sir, tell it to me."

Part 3

1. "Mind is beyond speech,
For as a closed fist
Holds two acorns,
Two gooseberries,
Two walnuts,
Two figs,
So does mind
Hold both speech and name.
If a man is minded to read
The Sacred Books

He reads them.
Similarly if minded
To perform actions,
To wish for sons,
Great herds of cattle,
To possess this world
And the other,
If God be willing
He gets his wish.
For mind is in the Self,
Mind creates the world,
Mind is in Brahman,
Meditate on 'That'.

Without the instrument of reason, a mental capacity rooted in the brain, Self cannot act in or enjoy the divine play, as *lila*, the drama of life.

2. He who meditates
    On reason as Brahman
    Is Lord and Master
    As far as reason goes."
    "Sir, is there something
    Beyond the mind of reason?"
    "Yes."
    "Sir, please tell me."

Part 4

1. "Will[77] is beyond reason,
    When a man or woman wills
    He or she thinks from his reason,
    Then he or she speaks with names.
    In a name all sacred hymns
    Are contained,
    In the sacred hymns
    All sacrifices.

2. All these beginning with reason and mind
    Ending in sacrifice,[78]
    Centre in will,
    Consist of will,
    Rest in will.
    Heaven and Earth willed
    Air,
    Ether,
    Water,
    Fire,
    All willed.
    Through the will
    Of heaven and Earth
    Rain wills
    And food wills,
    Through the will of food

The vital Life Breath wills,
The sacred hymns will,
The sacrifices will.
Through the will
Of the world
All wills.
This is will.
Meditate on will.

3. He or she who meditates
On will
As Brahman,
He or she being safe,
Firm,
Stress-free,
Obtains that which he or she wills.
He or she is Lord and Master
As far as will reaches
He or she who meditates
On will
As Brahman."
"Sir, is there something
Beyond the will?"
"Yes."
"Please tell it to me, Sir."

Part 5

1. "Consideration is better than will.
   When a man or woman
   Considers, then he wills,
   Then he thinks in his mind,
   Then he speaks,
   He names.
   In a name the sacred hymns are contained
   And all sacrifices.

2. All these starting with mind
   Ending in sacrifice,
   Centre, consist, abide,
   In consideration.
   If a man is inconsiderate
   Even if erudite
   People reject him as worthless.
   If a man is considerate
   They listen gladly
   Even if he knows very little!
   Consideration is centred,
   It is in the Self,
   It is the support of all this,
   Meditate on consideration.

3. He who meditates
   On consideration as Brahman
   Is safe, firm, unstressed,
   And reaches those worlds
   And is Lord and Master
   As far as consideration reaches."
   "Sir, is there something better
   Than consideration?"
   "Yes."
   "Tell it to me then."

Part 6

1. "Reflection is beyond consideration.
   When a man or woman reflects
   He or she wills,
   Then he thinks from reason,
   He speaks,
   He names,
   In names are the Vedas,
   In the Vedas are all austerities.

2. He who meditates
   On reflection as Brahman
   Is Lord and Master
   As far as reflection reaches."
   "Sir is there anything

Beyond reflection?"
"Yes."
"Sir, please tell me."

Part 7

1. "Understanding is beyond reflection.
   Through understanding
   We know all the Sacred Books,
   All the Sciences,
   All the Polarities,
   This world and 'That',
   So meditate on understanding.

2. He reaches the worlds
   Of understanding and cleverness
   Of understanding."
   "Sir, is there anything
   Beyond this?"
   "Yes."
   "Tell me then, please."

Part 8

"Power is beyond reflection.
One powerful man or woman
Shakes a hundred men of erudition.
If a man or woman
Becomes powerful he or she rises,
He or she visits the wise,
If he visits he or she becomes a follower of the
Wise.
If he follows the wise
He becomes
A seeing,
Hearing,
Perceiving,
Knowing,
Acting,
Understanding
Man or woman.
By power, our Earth stands firm,
As does the sapphire sky,
Emerald leaves,
Snow-capped mountains,
The Pantheon of Gods,
The society of mankind,
Herds of cattle,
Flocks of birds,

Green aromatic herbs,
Magnificent flowering trees,
Beasts of the jungle,
Worms of the soil,
Midges of the summer air,
Ants in their hill cities,
By power all stands firm
And strong."
"Is there anything
Beyond power?"
"Yes."
"Sir, please tell me."

Friedrich Nietzsche believed that the "Will to Power" was the answer to the universal riddle, and that the affirmation of "what is" by being a "yea-sayer" neutralized the narcissistic egotism.

Part 9

1. "Food is beyond power,
    If a man or woman fasts
    For ten days,
    Though he lives
    Slowly he fails to hear,
    Perceive,
    Think,

Act,
Understand.
When he is fed
All is restored.
Meditate on the miracle
Of food.

2. He who meditates on food
As Brahman
Reaches the worlds rich
In sustenance,
He is Lord and Master
As far as food reaches."
"Is there anything
Beyond this food?"
"Yes."
"Please tell me, Sir."

Part 10

"Water is beyond food.
If there is no rain
Vital spirits fail
From fear of famine.
With abundant rain
Vital spirits rejoice
Because there will be good harvest.

Water transforming
Becomes Earth,
Sky,
Heaven,
Mountains,
Gods,
Men,
Women,
Cattle,
Birds,
Herbs,
Trees,
Beasts,
Reptiles,
Insects.
So meditate on water.
He who meditates on water
As Brahman
Obtains his wishes,
He becomes satisfied,
He is Lord and Master
As far as the waters reach."
"Is there something
Beyond water?"
"Yes."
"Sir, tell me."

Part 11

1. "Fire is beyond water.
    Fire united with air
    Warms the ethereal space.
    People say, it is hot,
    It will soon rain.
    So fire creates water
    And thunderclaps come
    With lightning flashing
    Up and across the sky.
    It will soon rain
    So fire makes water.
    Meditate on fire.

2. He or she who meditates
    On fire as Brahman
    Obtains resplendent worlds,
    Full of light, free from darkness.
    He or she is Lord and Master
    As far as fire reaches,
    He or she who meditates
    On fire as Brahman."
    "Is there anything
    Beyond fire?"
    "Yes."
    "Please tell me, Sir."

Part 12

1. "Ethereal space is beyond fire,
   There lives Sun,
   Moon,
   Lightning,
   Galaxies
   And fire.[79]
   Through ethereal space we speak
   Hear, answer,
   Rejoice when together,
   Mourn when separated.
   In ethereal space
   All is born
   And towards ethereal space
   All tends,
   So meditate on ethereal space.

2. He who meditates
   On the grandeur of ethereal space
   As Brahman
   Gains the worlds of ether and light,
   Free from pressure and pain,
   Wide and all embracing.
   He or she is Lord
   And Master as far as ethereal space reaches."
   "Sir, is something beyond ethereal space?"

"Yes."
"Please tell me, Master."

Part 13

1. "Memory[80] is beyond even ethereal space.
   When many are gathered together
   If they had no memory
   They would not understand language,
   They would not perceive.
   Through memory, we recognize
   Our family and friends,
   We also, by memory, number our herds.
   Meditate on memory.

2. He or she who meditates
   On memory as Brahman
   Is as it were Lord and Master
   As far as memory goes."
   "Sir, is there anything beyond this precious
   Gift of memory?"
   "Yes indeed."
   "Please then tell me, Sir."

Part 14

1. "Hope is beyond memory.
   Fired by hope
   Memory reads the Vedas,
   Performs sacred acts,
   Wishes for sons and cattle,
   This world and the other.
   Meditate on hope.

2. He who meditates
   On Brahman as hope,
   His prayers are answered,
   He or she is Lord and Master
   As far as hope can go."
   "Sir, is there anything
   Beyond hope?"
   "Yes, Narada."
   "Please tell it to me then."

Part 15

1. "Spirit is beyond hope.
   As the wheel spokes hold to the rim
   So does all this hold from words
   Of hope to spirit.

That spirit moves by spirit,
It gives spirit to spirit,
Spirit is father,
Mother,
Sister,
Brother,
Teacher,
Brahmin.

2. For if one says any words
Unbecoming to father,
Mother,
Brother,
Sister,
Tutor,
A Brahmin,
Shame!
You have offended them.

3. But if after the spirit
Leaves the body
One puts them all together
On a funeral pyre
No one would say
You have offended them.

4. Spirit is all 'That',
    He who sees and understands 'That'
    Becomes a master of disputation.
    If people say to such a man or woman
    'You are a master of disputation,'
    He or she need not deny it.

Part 16

But in reality
He is a true Master
Who declares
The Supreme Being, Brahman
To be the Truth, Consciousness,
Reality, Love."
"My guru, may I become
A Master of 'That' Truth?"
"But we must earnestly wish
To know 'That'."
"Sir, I desire to know 'That'."

Part 17

"When one understands the True
As Consciousness
One declares the Truth.
One who does not understand 'That'

Does not declare the Truth.
For understanding
We must wish to understand."
"Sir, I wish to understand
'That'."

Part 18

"When one apperceives
One understands,
For this apperception
We must wish
To understand."
"Sir, I wish to understand."

Part 19

"When one has great faith
One apperceives
But by this faith we must wish
To understand."
"Sir, I fail to understand."

Part 20

"When one listens
With attention
To a true guru
Then one has faith
And resonance.
One who fails to pay attention
Does not have faith
But this attention we must understand."
"I desire to understand it, Sir."

Part 21

"When one practises
Restraint of the senses,
Concentration of the mind,
Then one really pays attention
To the guru.
These practices we must wish to understand."
"Sir, I wish to understand them."

Part 22

"When one feels peace in oneself
It is because of paying
Full attention to the Self.
This peace we must wish to understand."
"Please tell me, Sir."

Part 23

"The Infinite Brahman,
The resonance with the guru,
Consciousness to Consciousness,
Brings peace.
There is no peace in finite things
But Infinity we must wish to understand."
"I wish to understand, Master,
Please tell me."

Part 24

1. "When one sees nothing
   Other than no-thing,
   Understands no-thing,
   'That' is Infinite.
   When ones sees something else
   Than no-thing,

Hears something else,
Understands something else,
That is finite.
The Infinite is Eternal,
The finite dies."
"Sir in what does
The Infinite rest?"
"In its own grandeur
Or not even in grandeur.[81]

2. In the world
They call milking cattle,
Chariot horses,
Load-bearing elephants,
Faithful wives,
Ploughed fields,
Well-built houses,
Grandeur.
I do not mean
Any of this
For then the possessor
Rests in his possessions,
But the Infinite cannot rest
In something different
From Infinity itself.

Part 25

1. Infinity is below,
   Above,
   Behind,
   Before,
   Right,
   Left,
   All 'That'.
   The Infinite is the I-I,
   I-I am below,
   Above,
   Inside,
   Behind,
   Before,
   Right,
   Left,
   I-I am all 'That'.

The "I-I" is a way of expressing the plenary experience of pure Consciousness or Self in the core of one's being, the heart. It is not the "I" of imagined individuality. This "I-I" is the essential "I-am-ness", not "I went for a walk", etc.

2. The Infinite
   Is the Self of Consciousness
   Below,
   Above,

Behind,
Before,
Inside,
Right,
Left,
Consciousness, Self, is all 'That'.
He who sees,
Apperceives,
Understands
'That'
Loves the Self,
Delights in Consciousness,
Rests in Peace
He becomes a Self-Ruler,
Lord and Master
In all worlds,
But those who think
Differently from 'That'
Live in perishable worlds
And are governed over
By their rulers,
Usually tyrants.

Part 26

1. To he or she who sees,
   Apperceives,
   Understands,
   That the spirit,
   Hope,
   Memory,
   Ethereal space,
   Fire,
   Water,
   Birth,
   Death,
   Food,
   Power,
   Reflection,
   Will,
   Mind,
   Speech,
   Names,
   Hymns,
   Austerities,
   All spring from the Self
   Of Consciousness, Awareness, Peace,

2. There is a verse:
   He who sees 'That'
   Does not know death,
   Illness,
   Pain,
   He who sees 'That'
   Sees all and obtains all.
   He is One before creation,
   He becomes three,
   Fire,
   Water,
   Earth,
   He becomes five, seven, nine,
   Eleventh, a hundred and ten,
   One thousandth and twenty,
   The endless varieties of name and form.
   When the intellect is purified
   The whole nature is pure,
   The memory is twin
   And when the Self of Consciousness
   Is constantly remembered
   Then all the bonds of ignorance are released."
   So the venerable sage
   Sanatkumara
   Taught Narada

After removing his attachment
To worldly knowledge alone.
They call Sanatkumara
Skanda,[82] yes Skanda.

BOOK VIII

Part 1

1. "Harihi AUM
   There is this city of Brahman,
   A palace,
   The small lotus flower
   Of the Heart
   And in 'That' ethereal space,
   What is to be sought, traced,
   To be understood?

2. And if they should ask,
   'Now regarding this city
   Of Brahman
   And its Ethereal Palace
   How is it to be understood?'

3. As large as all space
   Is the ether within the Heart.[83]
   Heaven and Earth are
   Contained,
   Fire,
   Air,
   Sun,
   Moon,

Lightning,
Stars,
Whatsoever is of the Self
In the world
And whatever is not,
All 'That' is contained.

4. If all that exists
    Is in this city,
    All beings,
    Their desires,
    Then what is left
    When old age reaches
    And scatters 'That'?

5. By body senility
    The ether does not age,
    By death,
    The ether is not stained,
    'That' is the true city,
    Not the body.
    In it all desires are held,
    It is the Self, Consciousness,
    Sinless,
    Ageless,
    Deathless,
    Griefless,

Hunger free,
Desiring nothing
But what it needs to desire,[84]
Imagines nothing
But what it ought to imagine.
Now as on Earth
Folk follow as ordained
Dependent on a nation or land.

6. As on Earth
Whatever has been gained
By effort perishes.
So dies, whatever is
Acquired for the next world
By austerities,
And so-called good deeds.
Those who leave from here
Without knowing the Self,
As Consciousness, Reality,
Love,
Will not find freedom
In any world.
But those who leave
After knowing the Self
As Consciousness,
For them is freedom
In all worlds.

Part 2

This chapter deals with obtaining the different varieties of heavenly worlds and is omitted. This is the *apara vidya* or exoteric teaching. To the Advaitin the question of lower or higher worlds is largely irrelevant as mental projection.

Part 3

Verse 1 refers to the previous chapter.

1. These desires for other worlds,
    However sincere,
    Are hidden by a false veil.
    Whoever belongs to us has left this life
    And cannot be gained back
    For us to see him or her again.

2. Those who belong to us,
    Whether living or dead,
    And all we wish for
    And all that we do not reach
    And all that we find if we delve deeply
    Into the Heart where Brahman dwells
    In the ethereal space;
    But they cannot be seen with the eyes.
    Just as those who do not know the land

Ramble again and again
Over a gold treasure
Hidden in the Earth
And never find it,
So do all beings sink
Into Brahman
When asleep,
Yet never find it
Because they are deceived
By illusion and never find
The 'That' dwelling in the Heart.

3. The Self of Consciousness,
Reality, Love,
Lives in the Heart.
The Heart is called
Hridayam,
He 'Who Is' in the Heart.
He who knows 'That'
Goes when in deep sleep
Into the heaven of Brahman
In the Heart.

Chapter II of the *Ramana Gita* discusses the science of the heart, central to Ramana Maharshi's teaching.

4. Now that serene Being
   Which arises
   From the body
   After reaching the light
   Of Self-Knowledge
   Appears in its true form,
   Pure Consciousness.
   This is the Immortal;
   The fearless, Brahman,
   'That is Truth'
   Sattyam.

5. Sattyam
   Means Sat
   The Immortal,
   Tyam the mortal,
   Yam binds both.
   He who understands 'That'
   Enjoys the heavenly bliss
   Of Brahman.

Part 4

1. 'That' Self of Consciousness,
   Reality, Love,
   Is like a river bank,
   A boundary, an edge,

So that the worlds may not be confused.
Day and night do not cross that bank
Nor old age death,
Suffering,
Good or evil deeds,
Wicked ones reject 'That'.
The world of Brahman
Is free from all evil.

2. He who crosses over the river
By the raft of this teaching,
If blind, ceases to be blind,
If wounded in mind or body,
Ceases to be wounded,
If afflicted, ceases to be afflicted.
So when the river has been crossed,
The night of ignorance becomes the day
Of awakening,
The world of Brahman
Is illumined once and for all.

3. 'That' world of Brahman
Belongs to all those
Who find it by abstaining
From mind wandering
And outrageous passions.
For them there is freedom!
In all worlds."

Parts 5 and 6

Parts 5 and 6 are omitted – Part 5 is largely about sacrificial minutiae and Part 6 deals with the colours of heart arteries and the mechanics of death following from this.

Part 7

1. Prajapati said,
   "The Self of Consciousness,
   Reality, Love,
   Is free from sin,
   Senility,
   Death,
   Grief,
   Hunger,
   Thirst,
   Desires,
   And imagines nothing
   But what is needful.
   'That it is'
   We must seek,
   Enquire,
   Study,
   Trace,
   Search,
   Understand.

Then he obtains all worlds
And wishes."

2. The Gods and Demons
    Overheard his words
    And said,
    "Well let us do
    What he commands."
    So Indra went
    From the Gods,
    Virokana from the Demons,
    And both unknowingly
    To the other
    Approached Prajapati,
    Bearing fuel as was the custom
    For pupils coming to a Master.

3. They stayed as pupils
    For thirty-two years.
    Then Prajapati asked,
    "Why have you both come
    Here and stayed so long?"
    They answered,
    "We have heard you say
    The Self of Consciousness,
    Reality, Love,
    Is free from sin,

Senility,
Grief,
Hunger,
Thirst,
Desires,
And imagines nothing
But what is needful.
That it is which we
Must see,
Enquire,
Study,
Trace,
Search,
Understand.
Then we will obtain
All worlds and wishes.
Now both of us have come
Because we wish for 'That'."
Prajapati replied, "The Supreme in the eye,
The real agent of seeing,
'That' is the Self.
This is what I have said,
This is Immortal, fearless,
Brahman, Consciousness."
They asked,
"But that which is seen
In the water

As a reflection
Or in a mirror,
What is that?"
Prajapati answered,
"'That' indeed is seen
In all these too."

There is no duality in the Self; all is Consciousness,
Consciousness is all there is; the substratum is of every
combination of atoms, elements, etc. As Brahman is the
ground of the phenomenal world, samsara becomes nirvana
when duality vanishes through grace.

Part 8

1. "Gaze at your face
   In a bowl of water
   And whatever you
   Do not understand
   About the Self as Consciousness
   Please tell me?"
   They looked.
   Prajapati asked them
   What they saw.
   "We both see the face,
   A picture even to the very hairs and spots."

2.   Prajapati said to them,
     "After you have dressed,
     Made yourselves up,
     Washed, look again.
     Now what do you see?"

3.   "Just as we are
     At this moment."
     "That reflection is the Self."
     They both left satisfied
     Trusting Prajapati.

4.   Prajapati thought,
     "They both leave
     Without having seen the Real Self
     And whoever Devil or God
     Believes this false doctrine will perish."
     Virokana, pleased, told the Devils
     That the body is to be
     Worshipped,
     That is the Self.

5.   So any man who fails
     To give alms,
     Who has no path,
     Offers no austerities
     Is a Devil, for this is their doctrine.

They deck out the bodies of the dead
With perfumes, flowers, fine clothes
And worship these bodies to conquer the next
World.
This was the fundamental error of the Ancient
Egyptians.

Part 9

1. But Indra, King of the Gods,
   Saw the difficulty,
   "This so-called Self,
   A shadow in the body
   Will die when the body dies,
   I do not follow this false teaching."

2. He again went to see
   Prajapati.
   After traditional greetings
   Prajapati asked him why he
   Had returned?

3. Indra said,
   "This so-called Self in the water
   Is only the body,
   It will die when the body dies."

4.   Prajapati said, "Good,
      Well I shall explain
      The nature of the True Self,
      Stay with me
      Another thirty-two years."

Thirty-two years seems to be an auspicious time. Both Jesus
and Shankara only lived thirty-two years on the planet.

Part 10

1.   Prajapati informed Indra
      After thirty-two years, and said,
      "That Consciousness
      Which moves about happily in dreams,
      'That' is the Self,
      The Immortal,
      Fearless, Brahman."

2.   Indra was somewhat satisfied
      But before returning
      To the Gods he saw a difficulty,
      "But although it is true,
      The Self of Consciousness is not blind
      Even if the body is blind,
      Nor is the Self affected
      By the faults of the body,

Nor struck when the body is struck,
Nor wounded when the body is wounded.
It is as if they really struck
The Self as in dreams,
As if they chased 'That'
He becomes aware
Of pain and the body cries out.
I see no good in this."

3. He returned to Prajapati
   And told him his objection.

4. "So be it," replied Prajapati.
   "Stay here another thirty-two years
   And I will tell you."
   He stayed another thirty-two years.
   Prajapati said:

Part 11

1. "When a man or woman
   Is deeply asleep,
   Dreamless,
   At perfect rest,
   That is Consciousness,
   Self,
   Immortal,

Fearless,
Brahman."

2. Indra was deeply satisfied,
But before returning
To the Gods
He saw a difficulty.
In truth he does not know
His Self,
Who this I is
And "That" he is I-I,
Nor that anything real exists.
He is utterly annihilated.
He sees no good in this.

3. Again he goes to see
Prajapati.
Prajapati asks him
"Why do you need to come back
After appearing satisfied?"

4. "Sir," he said,
"I am confused,
From what you say
One does not know his Self,
That he is I-I,
Or who I is,
And whether anything exists."

"I-I" is the plenary experience of the Self. The "I" is the functional ego. "Nothing really exists" is the absolute advanced teaching of Advaita, because the world dream is maya or illusion.

5. "So it is indeed,
    Lord Indra.
    But live here
    For five more years.
    I shall tell you all."

Part 12

1. After five years
    Prajapati said,
    "This body is mortal
    And always held by death,
    Yet it is a home
    For 'That' Self of Consciousness,
    Immortal, bodiless.
    When in the body,
    By realizing
    This body is I
    And I am the body
    The Self is held in bondage
    By pleasure and pain,
    Like and dislike,[85]

But when he realizes
He is not the body,
That he is Consciousness, Reality, Love,
The Self, 'That', Brahman,
Then neither worldly pain
Nor pleasure
Holds him captive.

2. The wind is bodiless,
So are the clouds,
Lightning,
Thunder.
As these arise
From ethereal space
They appear in their own form
On reaching the highest light.

3. So does the Self,
The serene Consciousness,
Arising from this body
Appear in its own
Transparency,
Container of all that happens
In the highest light,
The Knowledge of Self.
In that state he is
The High Supreme,

He moves there spontaneously,
Appropriately,
Laughing,
Eating,
Celebrating,
Be it with men, women,
Relatives,
Chariots,
Never troubled by that body
Into which he was born.
Like the horse
Attached to the chariot,
So is the Conscious Self,
Attached to this body.
The body is in the Self.

4. Where the sight
Enters the void of the black pupil,
There is the Supreme of the eye.
The eye itself the instrument of seeing.
The same with the nose,
The agent of smelling.
As is the tongue, of speaking,
The ear, of hearing.
He who recognizes 'That'
As Truth is the Self.

5. He who understands 'That',
   Let him realize the reason is a Divine Eye.
   It perceives not only 'what is'
   Present but past and future
   And guides action.
   He, 'That Self', seeing
   These treasures
   Which to others are hidden and veiled,
   Rejoices in gratitude.
   The Gods in the state of Brahman
   Meditate on the Self
   As Pure Consciousness
   So all worlds are theirs
   As with all who know the Self."

Part 13

A Hymn of Triumph
Celebration of Self-Knowledge
From the darkness of my Heart
I came to the rebellious ego,
Shaking off evil
As a horse shakes his mane
As the Moon frees herself
From the mouth of Death's angel.[86]
Having shaken off
The foolish notion

That I am the corpse of a body,
I reached the fullness
Of the unborn, uncreated
World of the Self,
Brahman, Love, Consciousness,
Awareness, Peace.

Part 14

"That" which is called
The vast, Infinite
Ethereal space
Reveals all forms and names.
"That" in which these
Are contained
Is Brahman or Consciousness,
Immortal, Self.
Humbly I attend the hall
Of Prajapati's mansion.
I am glorious amongst Brahmins,
Amongst Princes,
Amongst men and women
Of all vocations.
I touched that glory,
I am glorious
Amongst the glorious.
May I never, ever, now descend

To the white, toothless,
But devouring abode
Of decadence.
May I never, ever go to it.

Part 15

Brahman gave this
Upanishad to Prajapati,
Prajapati to Manu,
Manu[87] to mankind.
He who has learned the Vedas
From a lineage of Teachers
According to the sacred rule,
After performing service to the guru,
Became a responsible householder,
Rekindling the memory of the teaching,
Fathered virtuous sons,
Concentrated on the Self
As Consciousness,
Never hurting any creature,
Who so behaves all his life
Reaches the world of Brahman
And never returns,
Yes he never returns.

NOTES

[1] Ramakrishna Vedanta Centre, Bourne End, Buckinghamshire.

[2] *The Upanishads*, Penguin Books.

[3] Faber & Faber Ltd.

[4] Ramana Maharshi often told questioners that worship of the form would eventually lead to worship of the formlessness, from His compassion.

[5] One is reminded of the atomic bomb.

[6] In Vedic times this was a secret knowledge. In modern times, through divine Grace, it has become an "open secret".

[7] The necklace of jewels is a symbol of the universe. To quote Ramesh Balsekar, the Mumbai Sage, "The Universe is uncaused, like a necklace of jewels in which each is only the reflection of all the others in a fantastic interrelated harmony without end."

[8] A definition of sin according to Dr. Maurice Nicol was "to miss the mark".

[9] The Buddha was tempted by pleasures before his enlightenment, as was Christ by power.

[10] Our real nature or Self is the Consciousness animating us. Our mind-body system is an object in that Consciousness playing a predestined role in the game of life. We see, hear, taste, feel, touch, etc. from this Consciousness; this is the message of these important verses.

[11] See my *Transcreation of the Bhagavad Gita* (O Books, John Hunt Publishing, 2003).

[12] Shankara comments: "The number of bricks for the fire altar should be 720 approximately, the number of days and nights added together." A brilliant exposition of the esoteric significance of the place of "fire" in Vedic mythology is to be found in Sri Aurobindo's introduction to *Hymns of Mystic Fire*.

[13] Lord Krishna as the Self was the charioteer for Arjuna (the spiritual seeker in the Gita). Lack of mental control leads to violence and anger.

[14] Somerset Maugham's masterpiece, *The Razor's Edge*, took its title from this verse. Maugham visited Ramanasramam and met the Maharshi as essential research for this great novel.

[15] This metaphor comes from the Rig Veda IV. 40:5. The swan swimming in the lake is the Parahamsa swimming in the lake of bhakti. Hence the name given to Ramakrishna, the Supreme Sannyasin.

[16] The branches fall down and take root forming new stems. The fifteenth chapter of the Bhagavad Gita expands this metaphor of the Tree of Life. Brahman is then anthropomorphized on a cosmic level, transcendent as well as immanent. Many theosophies and mythologies, for example the Hebrew Kabbalah and Norse mythology, give importance to the Tree of Life.

[17] The ethereal angels are the beautiful Gandharvas.

[18] There is no Teacher without a pupil. The guru is in the resonance that arises between them. In the understanding they become One. The Teacher may also be the Sat-Guru in the heart, or even a sacred mountain, as Arunachala was to Sri Ramana Maharshi.

[19] "Svaha" is a Vedic interjection between each prayer.

[20] "Suvas", "Bhu", and "Bhuvas" are the Yajur Veda's invocations. These verses permutate sacred words with different meanings.

[21] Brahman is not an object, it is the ultimate subject.

[22] Intellectual understanding alone is insufficient. The heart must also open.

[23] The form of mankind is similar to the Platonic archetype of man or the Universal Man, the Adman Kadman of the Kabbalah. The subtle or evolved intellect is above the normal common power of conceptual reasoning. Reason cannot reach the numinous or metaphysical world – but "That" may descend as an experience to assure the aspirant of the Truth.

[24] Gandharvas are famed for their beauty of form and purity.

[25] Mahatma is a "great soul", an honorific title later bestowed on Gandhi.

[26] To teach by silence is very rare even amongst sages. Ramana Maharshi is the most recent to do so.

[27] Maharshi means "Great Rishi", a rare honorific term.

[28] Bhagavan literally means "Godlike", another rare honorific term.

[29] The Primeval Sage who taught by silence was Dakshinamurti.

[30] A priestly Vedic god of the supreme rank, Lord of Speech. His Sutras have unfortunately been lost. Prof. Radhakrishna suspects his doctrine was materialist, denying existence after the death of the body. But other commentators believe he was not a materialist but knew that the

egoistic entity does not exist after death. The subtle body transmigrates after death, returning first to Source. Source then transfers the subtle body with others to make any new body it wishes to act in the great divine drama.

31 A synonym of Brahma, creator god.

32 This could also refer to the Shiva linga, symbol of the life force, sacred to the Vedic tradition.

33 Esoterically his "inner foes" are the doubting voices in himself. This is echoed in the Book of Psalms that also castigates enemies, the negative inner dialogue of despair and depression.

34 In Jewish mysticism, Kabbalah also means Secret Tradition.

35 Shankara on Aitareya III. 1:1.

36 Rig Veda VIII. 101:14

37 Succour can be understood as divine grace on which all depend.

38 As a master lives by his servants and his servants live by him – Max Weber.

39 Heart here may be interpreted as Consciousness, the space wherein everything happens.

40 The belly here is the navel or Buddhist "hara".

41 Rig Veda VIII. 92:32

42 The Silver Age was the time of the Vedic culture in the Saraswati Valley. Now we are in the Kali Yuga (the Iron Age), an age of gross materialism where higher knowledge is scattered not collected.

43 Ghee is clarified butter, used in Hindu ritual ceremonials.

44 This metaphor reappears in the Katha Upanishad II:5. Christ called those without spiritual insight "the blind".

45 "The sparks fly up" is a metaphor also used in the Jewish mystical tradition.

46 Cause and effect, along with time, space, and colour, are s"a priori" in the brain, the organ of cognition. This was logically and observationally proved by Immanuel Kant and Arthur Schopenhauer. See *The Critique of Pure Reason* (Kant) and *The Fourfold Root of the Principle of Sufficient Reason* (Schopenhauer). These precepts create the maya in which the world plan (or dream) is enacted.

47 Published by Advaita Ashrama, trans. Swami Gambhivananada. There is also an excellent commentary on this Upanishad by Swami Krishnananda published by the Divine Life Society, 1997.

48 These are described in the Chandogya Upanishad section V.18:2.

[49] This is the view of most mystics: "all is good". Julian of Norwich, being an exemplary teacher, said: "All is well, very, very, very well." It must be because all flows from God; what we call "wicked" is a dissonant note in the cosmic harmonious balance. "Suffering leads to God realization," said Ramana Maharshi. Evil is an anthropomorphic concept, which ignores the divine will to maintain equilibrium.

[50] Refers to the Source of creation.

[51] The cosmic Purusa.

[52] The sacrificial fire during the Horse Sacrifice (Deussen).

[53] Soma, the God of Inspiration is akin to Dionysus or Bacchus in ancient Greece, the God of Intoxicants. The Soma "intoxicant" lifted men to an elevated state. The soma plant was deified and used in sacrifices. The exact identification of the hallucinogenic plant has been lost to posterity. For further detail see *Indian Philosophy* Vol 1 pages 83–4 by S. Radhakrishnan. In this verse soma could be read alternatively simply as a divine drink. Brahman becomes Brahma in his role as Creator God.

[54] A Vedic koan.

[55] Ecstasy.

[56] A purple red dye from Cochin in India. It is the blood of a crushed female scaly beetle.

[57] This is the procedure of *neti neti*, whereby the continual denial of what appears reveals "what is". "That" which is left after all else is negated. It is a Buddhist device used in the *Via Negativa*. J. Krishnamurti favoured *neti neti*. Vedanta is mainly the *Via Positiva*, the exposition of "what is" rather than "what is not".

[58] Most spiritual teachers point out that extreme wealth is a severe obstacle to spiritual progress. Jesus of Nazareth stressed this over and over again.

[59] Honey is a mysterious substance. The excretion of a social insect, the bee, gathered from flowers, it is a boon to mankind, with many uses, as a food and medicine.

[60] The simile of honey is to indicate the 'sweet inner essence'. A similar use is made in the Old Testament, journeying to the Promised Land – Canaan – the land of 'milk and honey'.

[61] Dharma, the way of law of righteousness.

[62] Translated by Swami Swahananda of the Sri Ramakrishna, Malts, Madras, 1980.

⁶³ Dharma.

⁶⁴ The Gayatri Mantra is the most sacred verse in the Rig Veda; it has immense potency.

⁶⁵ Atman or Purusha.

⁶⁶ Gently pressing the closed eyelids reveals the inner light. Self-Enquiry here would be "Who sees the light?"

⁶⁷ That men and women are creatures of will anticipates the philosophy of the 19th-century German Transcendental Idealists such as Schopenhauer who had read the Upanishads. See *World as Will and Idea*, Arthur Schopenhauer.

⁶⁸ Jesus also analogously used the mustard seed as a symbol of the Kingdom of Heaven.

⁶⁹ Purusha.

⁷⁰ The Vaisvanara Self is the teaching of Self understood by the Vishnaic teaching, and is limited according to this Upanishad.

⁷¹ "Cloud Messenger" is the title of a poem by Kalidas set beautifully as a choral work by Gustav Holtz, a Sanskrit scholar, who also set Rig Veda Hymns, composed an opera, *Rama and Sita*, as well as a chamber opera, *Savitri*. Today he is more famed for his *Planets Suite*.

⁷² See my anthology *The Wisdom of Ramesh Balsekar* for further elucidation, Watkins Publishing, 2003.

⁷³ Probably Kandahar.

⁷⁴ Narada later became a legendary rishi of great power. He composed the famous *Bakti Sutras*, teaching the way of devotion through surrender, which led to Self-Realization. Here he is taught by the sage Sanatkumara.

⁷⁵ Ramana Maharshi often referred to science as learned ignorance. Scientists are interpreting maya most of the time.

⁷⁶ The world illusion is based on apparent polarities. One can witness this in one's own psyche. Time, space, and causality are "a priori" in the brain (organ of cognition) and do not really exist except as conveniences for interpreting the man-created phenomenal world. Each animal has its own universe. Man is a species in nature, as much as any other creature, except he has the gift of reason.

⁷⁷ The nature of the will is an important theme in Western Transcendental Idealist Philosophy, as is the nature of reason. Kant's *Critique of Pure Reason* was seminal in modern Western philosophy.

78 For modern man austerity could be better understood than sacrifice. Alternatively the word *surrender* could be used.

79 Agni.

80 Without memory everything would be as if it were not, as far as the human being is concerned.

81 Nothing or no-thing in a world of everything is a paradox for the empiric mind to try to understand: an Advaitic koan. By being nothing one is space for everything.

82 Skanda was the youngest son of Lord Shiva born to slay the demon Taraka. Symbolically Taraka is the demon of human egotism, which prevents Self-Knowledge. Ramana Maharshi was called Skanda by the Tamil poet-sage, Ganapati Muni.

83 The ether in the heart may be understood as Brahman.

84 Basic bodily needs.

85 The "I am the body idea" is the mistaken identification which enslaves the human being.

86 Rahu, a monster who swallows the sun and moon at the time of eclipses.

87 Manu was the author of the Laws which governed the Vedic civilization.

BIBLIOGRAPHY

Aurobindo, Sri, *The Upanishads* (Pondicherry: Aurobindo Ashram Trust, 1992)

Deussen, Paul, *Sixty Upanishads of the Rig Veda* (2 Vols), tr. V. M. Bedekar & G. B. Palsule (Delhi: Motilal Banarsidass, 1990)

Deussen, Paul, *The Philosophy of The Upanishads*, tr. A. S. Geddes (Dover, 1966)

Easwaran, Eknath, *The Upanishads* (Arkana, 1988)

Frawley, David, *The Rig Veda* (New Delhi: Aditya Prakashan)

Frawley, David, *Gods, Sages & Kings* (New Delhi: Motilal Banarsidass)

Frawley, David, *Wisdom of the Ancient Seers* (Lotus Press, 1993)

Gambhirananda, Swami, tr., *Eight Upanishads Vols I & II* (Advaita Ashrama, 1989)

Gambhirananda, Swami, tr., *Svetasvatara Upanishad* (Advaita Ashrama, 1986)

Krishnananda, Swami, *Mandukya Upanishad: An Exposition* (Divine Life Society, 1981)

Macnicol, Nicol, ed., *Hindu Scriptures* (Everyman, 1938)

Madhavananda, Swami, *The Brihadaranyaka Upanishad* (Calcutta: Advaita Ashrama, 1993)

Mascaro, Juan, tr., *The Upanishads*, (London: Penguin Classics, 1965)

Muller, Max, tr., *The Upanishads Vols I & II* (Dover, 1962)

Pandit, M. P., *Glossary of Sanskrit Terms* (Pondicherry: Aurobindo Ashrama, 1966)

Prabhavananda, Swami & Frederick, *The Upanishads* (Manchester: Mentor, 1948)

Radhakrishnan, S., *Indian Philosophy Vol I & Vol II* (Delhi: OUP, 1923)

Radhakrishnan, S., *The Principal Upanishads* (Delhi: OUP, 1953)

Sarma, Sri Lakshmana, *Maha Yoga or The Upanishadic Lore in the Light of the Teaching of Bhagavan Sri Ramana Maharshi* (Tiruvannamalai: Ramanasraman, 1973)

Shankaranarayanan, *Bhagavan and Nayana* (Tiruvannamalai: Ramanasramam, 1997)

Shearer, Alistair, *The Upanishads* (Unwin, 1989)

Sivananda, Swami, *The Yoga Vedanta Dictionary* (Divine Life Society, 1951)

Swahananda, Swami, *Chandogya Upanishad* (Madras: Sri Ramakrishna Matt, 1956)

Swami, Sri Purohisit & Yeats, W. B., *The Ten Principal Upanishads* (London: Faber, 1937)

Tyagisananda, Swami, *Svetasvatara Upanishad* (Madras: Sri Ramakrishna Matt)

Zaehner, R. C. & Dent, J. M. tr., *Hindu Scriptures* (1966)